D1258242

Everyday
Horsemanship

Everyday
Horsemanship

JESSAMINE COUNTY PUBLIC LIBRARY
600 South Main Street
Nicholasville, KY 40356
(859) 885-3523

Eliza R. L. McGraw

Sterling Publishing Co., Inc.

New York

Library of Congress Cataloging-in-Publication Data Available

10 9 8 7 6 5 4 3 2 1

Published by Sterling Publishing Co., Inc.
387 Park Avenue South, New York, NY 10016
© 2003 by Eliza R.L. McGraw
Distributed in Canada by Sterling Publishing
c/o Canadian Manda Group, One Atlantic Avenue, Suite 105
Toronto, Ontario, Canada M6K 3E7
Distributed in Great Britain by Chrysalis Books
64 Brewery Road, London N7 9NT, England
Distributed in Australia by Capricorn Link (Australia) Pty. Ltd.
P.O. Box 704, Windsor, NSW 2756, Australia

Printed in China
All rights reserved
Sterling ISBN 0-8069-8827-4

Unless otherwise noted, all photographs are by
Onawa M. Cutshall

Disclaimer

This book contains the opinions and ideas of its author. It is intended to provide helpful and inform-

ative material on the subject covered. It is sold with the understanding that the author and publisher

are not engaged in rendering professional services in the book. The reader should consult a compe-

tent professional for personal assistance or advice. The author and publisher specifically disclaim any

responsibility for any liability, loss, risk, personal or otherwise, which is incurred as a consequence,

directly or indirectly, of the use and application of any of the contents of this book.

3 2530 60584 4776

For Simon

Contents

Acknowledgments

Many thanks to the horses and riders who allowed themselves to be photographed for this book, and to the Maryland farm owners who provided the settings. These include Saddleview Ranch, Holly Hills Farm, Days End Farm Horse Rescue, the North Fork School of Equitation, Quiet Dawn Farm, the Damascus chapter of the Old People's Riding Club, and the home of Doris Kulp and Michael Rinehart.

I am very grateful to my family for supporting my riding and my writing, to my husband, Adam, for all his help, and to Madelyn Larsen, my agent and editor, who has seen this project through from the beginning.

Thanks to the people who have taught me about horses, cared for mine, and shared theirs with me: Vicky Haber, Sheri Tigue, George Sengstack, and especially Bruce Thompson.

And I am very indebted to all the horses I have known, particularly Romeo, who has taught me the most.

Introduction

The connection between people and horses is both ancient and timeless. Even as equestrian sports and disciplines change and grow, the tie remains secure. Horses are our teammates and employees, our partners and helpers and friends. We keep horses in our lives in a time when we no longer rely on them for transportation and labor, and riding is becoming more popular as horses serve new purposes in our lives.

The art of riding, keeping, and working with horses is called horsemanship, and involves much more than riding. Horsemanship itself, as an art independent of equestrian competition, is seeing a resurgence as some see horses as more than athletic partners. Horsemanship stems from true affection for horses. Some horsemen never ride, but enjoy horses in other ways. The word "horseman"—and many horsemen are women—describes a person who respects and understands horses and how to treat them. Horsemanship includes making decisions about the horses you care about. Piloting a hunter around a course of jumps is riding; realizing that he is hurt and pulling up before you're finished is horse-manship.

People become interested in horses for all kinds of reasons. Children as well as adults fall in love with the beauty and power horses exhibit, and some just realize all there is to be gained from time with horses. Many people get back into riding after a long time away from it. Dusty memories of barns and ponies call them back to riding lessons and stables as adults. And as those of us who ride know well, nothing compares to the combination of freedom and teamwork riding offers.

Today, many riders ride to compete. They spend their time with trainers and at horse shows, which can be a lot of fun, and certainly gratifying as the ribbons and standings begin to add up. Many of the greatest horsemen ride competitively, and seeing a real horseman succeed in the ring shows off the best of both horse and rider. But even as more people own horses, not all riders are turning to equestrian competition as their primary horsey pastime. Many people ride to relax, and cannot add one more stressful activity to their already hectic lives. Their horses represent a release from the rapid pace of the everyday, and riding a time of pure pleasure.

There is much we can teach horses, but also much that we can learn from them. You'll see grace when you watch your horse caper and arch deftly around a field. And while animal behaviorists may never be able to prove that horses can show affection or understanding for people, the forgiving nature of the hunter who takes a jump even as his rider grabs him in the mouth, or the patient pony who trucks child after child around an arena, demonstrate that they do much for us. We know how much we care about them; the least we can do is learn to care for them.

This is an exciting time to be in involved with horses. Ridership is high, and horsepeople are looking both forward and back as a general trend toward gentle methods of animal training has affected the horse world in new and innovative ways that simultaneously call on old traditions. This book is about learning to be a horseman. Those who grow up around horses often seem to come by it naturally; the rest of us need to learn. Nothing can replace time in the barn or the pasture, being there as horses eat and sleep, watching their daily lives and taking in their moment-to-moment existences. As you do that, read. This book will give you ideas about where to find horses, how to care for them, and all the different ways to enjoy them.

The way horses figure into our lives is constantly shifting. In a time where riding is a choice for most of us, we have the privilege of focusing on our relationships with horses instead of what they can pull or how far they can travel. There is a saying that horses get "in your blood," and that old saw feels true to anyone who loves horses, because we know how they become an intrinsic part of us and our daily lives, of our imagination, our actions, and our dreams.

Your **Horsemanship**
Goals

1

The world of horsemanship is always expanding. Whether it's endurance riding, cross-country riding, hunting, or vaulting, there are more choices in riding today than ever before. Many disciplines have spawned new sports and hobbies, from polocrosse to musical freestyle. And equestrians are constantly finding new ways to work horses into their other interests, like historical reenacting and photography.

Single-mindedness works for many riders. Some people (and horses) thrive on competing in one sport or discipline. Your love for endurance riding may eclipse other interests, and focus on a single sport is what helps make competitive champions. Yet too much focus can lead to frustration when riders discover that their horses don't fit the chosen discipline. Putting more money, effort, and time into a certain sport may or may not make it enjoyable or something at which you—or your horse— excel. Sometimes, changing direction can save you disappointment in yourself and your horse.

Also, horsemanship can benefit from versatility. Many of the best riders can switch between styles or sports with equal ease. You may have a favorite equestrian sport or type of riding, preferring the trail to the ring, or driving to getting in the saddle at all. But instead of wedding yourself only to one way of thinking and spending time with your horse, consider branching out. Go ahead and use that Western saddle to trail ride your hunter.

Diversifying goes against the current attitude. In a world where even some junior riders have equitation horses as well as jumpers to ride in various classes at shows, it's all too easy to classify our mounts. But unless you are competing at a high level, and need your horse to focus exclusively on his discipline, it can be good for both of you to work—and play—in different disciplines.

The choice available to riders today can become overwhelming. To figure out how you and your horse can keep your partnership energetic and fresh, set goals. Decide what you want for and from your horse. Why do you ride in the first place? Do you ride as a form of exercise? Do you ride to relax, or to motivate yourself to be outdoors? Do you enjoy the challenge of athletic competition? Do you ride to be with family members, or as an escape? Do you simply have, like so many of us, "horses in your blood," and can't imagine a life without them?

As your answers get more specific, so do the questions. Are you riding to participate in a sport with reliable demarcations and levels? Do you want to show locally? Or is your dream to take your horse on the national circuit? Is there a certain distance you want to cover on horseback?

Write these goals down. You may never want to show your list to anyone, but it helps to get your own ideas in order. If you realize that you are becoming frustrated with how much time you spend hacking and on the trail, for example, you may realize that you are ready to put more money and time into showing your horse. Preparing for a certain show will give you a measurable goal to work toward. On the other hand, are you spending too much time and money on lessons geared toward showing, and on shows themselves? You may want to look at your riding time and divide it into ring and trail time. Perhaps a goal for you would be a long trail ride, a pack trip, or even shifting your riding routine to two trail rides a week with two days spent in the arena.

Your Horse

Your horse, and his personality, will make a big difference in what your goals are. (For more on riding without your own horse, see Chapter 6, and for more on buying a horse, see Chapter 5). If you're shopping for a horse, you can work backwards and look for a horse who will best fit what you want. If you decide that you'd like to learn to jump, you may want a seasoned hunter who can help you reach that goal. If you're interested in trying your hand at driving, it may be easiest to find a horse who has done that before.

Horses are actually quite malleable as far as disciplines go. If you are not looking to compete at high levels, don't let breed or even conformation keep you from buying a horse you really like, or from keeping the one you have. It can be great fun to discover a hidden talent in your old partner. Your ring-sour show pony may be delighted to learn about the varied nature of the trail. And your trustworthy—albeit built "downhill" —Quarter Horse may be able to jump low courses just fine.

Don't be afraid to change your mind. Perhaps you had determined that you would learn to jump cross country. Then you realized that not only did you find it scary, but also your horse has little aptitude for it. Consider focusing on stadium jumping instead. That will give you the opportunity to jump in a more controlled environment. Although we all hear stories of horses who were born to do a certain sport, they're not in the majority. Most horses like variety, and even a horse who has spent years at one sport may be happy to try another.

Sport Options—A Selection

There is a wide range of equestrian sports to get involved in, whether you want to compete or simply to pick up a new hobby. Remember not to be bound by breed. While many endurance champions are Arabians, your Appaloosa may still be a good companion for endurance rides, especially if you're not competing. Don't pass up opportunities to watch a sports other than your own, whether at a local event or on television. Seeing other sports may inspire you to try something new.

Bear in mind that the sports described below just some of the horse sports available to you. These and other sports have their own variations and customs that are yours to discover as you become involved. New sports and disciplines are devised all the time, so don't let this brief list dissuade you from coming up with something entirely new that suits you and your horse.

Barrel Racing: Barrel racers ride at speed, performing patterns around barrels. They must get very close to the barrels without knocking them down, so their mounts, usually Quarter Horses, need to be deft as well as fast.

Calf Roping: Calf roping events include breakaway roping and ribbon roping. In breakaway roping, the rope is tied to the saddle horn. When the roped calf reaches the end of the rope, it breaks away from the horn and the run is complete. In ribbon roping, one person ropes a calf, then dismounts and holds the calf while her partner ties a ribbon to the calf's tail, then runs back across the starting line.

Competitive Trail Riding: This is similar to endurance riding, but not always so demanding. It is also more whole-horse oriented, with riders judged on equitation and their horse's manners as well as the speed at which they ride. The horses are also asked to navigate obstacles cleanly and without balking or spooking. Everything is judged, from turnout to what knot riders use to tie their horses with.

Cutting: This is a contest in which a horse and rider separate a particular cow from the herd, and the horse matches the cow's every move to keep it from returning to the herd. Cutting events are timed and judged by a point system which gives credits and penalties.

Dressage: Dressage is all about impulsion, collection, and flexion. Performing in an arena marked by a series of letters, dressage horses are trained to calibrate each motion precisely. Dressage is a serious and time-consuming sport, with riders practicing endlessly to achieve fluid and elegant movements from the extended walk to flying changes of lead at the higher levels of competition. Every horse can benefit from dressage because it maximizes their athletic abilities.

Driving: In this sport the horse is hitched to a carriage. Typically wheeled vehicles are pulled by one horse, two (called a pair), or four (four-in-hand). Driving sports include pleasure driving, tandem driving, four-in-hand, competitive distance carriage driving (which is a paced distance covering from 12 to 25 miles at about 6 or 7 miles an hour) and combined driving (which is like eventing for driven horses). In combined driving the dressage section tests the drivers on control, the marathon section tests the horses' stamina as they go over a long course, and the cones (or obstacle) section tests their ability to steer their horses through a complex course marked by cones.

Endurance Riding: This is long distance riding, usually over a varied terrain of fifty or more miles. Some rides span many days, and include shorter, 20 to 30 mile rides in their programs. Veterinarians check the horses at designated areas throughout the ride to make sure they are in good health. A horse showing stress or injury, for example, is not allowed to continue. Most endurance horses are Arabians, because the breed's built-in stamina and ability to deal with heat make it a natural. The winner is the horse and rider who finish first.

Equitation: In this sport the rider's style, turnout, and position are judged. The word equitation broadly means "horsemanship," especially as it influences skill at riding, but as a sport, equitation is focused on horse and rider under saddle.

Foxhunting: Foxhunting is the sport of chasing prey with a pack of hounds. Participation in this three-centuries-old

sport means membership in a highly structured and old-fashioned world that rewards members with tradition and a way of life. While all horse sports have their own lexicons and traditions, foxhunting may well have the most. Even if you do not wish to ride with the "first flight" or "first field," who keep up with the hounds, you can ride "second flight," or even "hilltop," which do not always involve jumping. Rules of attire are strict, and the social aspects of this highly organized sport are very important.

Gymkhana or Mounted Games: Pony-club aged riders tend to take part in such activities as pole bending, riding patterns around barrels, ring toss, the "rural route run" (which involves a mailbag), pairs classes in which two teams of two horses and riders hold a ribbon between them and follow instructions, relay races, egg-and-spoon races, and so forth.

Horseball: Horseball combines parts of both rugby and basketball on horseback. It is played at top speeds, with a lot of passing and shooting. Horseball is played between two teams of six riders who must pick up a ball from the ground without dismounting and, using a game of attack and defense, attempt to score in goals at each end of a pitch.

Hunters: Hunters are rated on their skill and style as well as speed and ability to clear fences. A hunter course is supposed to resemble the obstacles the horse would encounter in the hunt field.

Kür or Musical Freestyle: This is a dressage discipline. Taped music chosen by the rider is played while horse and rider "dance" to the music and show off the control, collection and athleticism of the team. Ideally, the performance exhibits gaits and movements timed to the music.

Polo: Polo is an ancient sport played by two teams of four riders each with the objective of scoring as many goals as possible. Players use mallets to strike a ball. The game, which is refereed, is divided into four or six periods called "chukkers." Because speed and contact are inherent, a break is taken between chukkkers in order for horses to be changed. Each horse may only be used for a maximum of two periods of play which may not be successive.

Polocrosse: Polocrosse is a combination of polo, lacrosse and netball. Two teams of six riders each use cane sticks with a loose twisted-thread net to carry and pass the ball and score goals. Polocrosse can also be played indoors in an arena.

Reining: Reiners, like dressage riders, have to complete a number of patterns, but in this sport, the patterns are based on those used in actual ranch work. Depending on the division, rollbacks, spins, and sliding stops are some of the displays.

Ride and Tie: Ride and tie comes from a time when two people sometimes needed to share one horse. One person rides down the trail, ties the horse, and starts running. The next person comes running down the trail, finds the horse, mounts, passing her partner, ties the horse at a specified location, and so on. Ride and tie is usually done at higher speeds than other trail sports as the riders race by their partners to save time.

Show or Stadium Jumping: Riders pilot their horses over jumps at speed, competing to see who can jump the obstacles without knocking a rail down, and who can do it the fastest. Knockdowns and refusals incur penalties called "faults." The rider with the fewest faults and the best time wins. Show jumping is for upper-level riders, because of the skill required to steer a horse around a complicated course, but jumping itself—at any height—can be a great deal of fun.

Team Roping: Partners, called a header (who ropes the steer around its head or neck) and a heeler (who ropes the steer around the hind feet), work together to rope and secure a steer in under fifteen seconds. The fastest time wins, with time added on due to infractions of the rules, such as catching only one of the steer's hind feet.

Team Penning: Cattle are put in teams of three, and herded to one end of an arena. The announcer calls out a number as the teams cross the starting line. The team separates the three head of cattle, pushes them to the other end of the arena, and pens them. The team with the best time wins.

Three-Day Eventing or Combined Training: This is an equestrian triathalon, with three sports combined in one: stadium jumping, dressage, and cross-country (a demanding ride over jumps on an outdoor course to be completed within a specified time.)

Trail Class: The basics of the trail class, designed to simulate obstacles you might encounter on the trail, often include walk-overs, artificial drops, bridges, water boxes,

Perfecting trail skills like opening a gate from horse-back improves rider and horse dexterity.

backing through obstacles, gates, and trotting and loping logs.

Vaulting: Vaulting is performing gymnastics on a moving horse. "Riders" wear leotards and the horse is on a longe line. Vaulting can be a team sport or an individual one.

Western Pleasure: In this sport, horses are judged by how comfortable and smooth their gaits are. Apparel is also key, with horses and riders wearing special coordinated ensembles, which are often flashy and decorative.

Hobby Aspect

Many of the hobbies that use horses offer amazing testimonials to the lengths people will go to ride. What follows is a sampling of possible hobbies, but ones involving horses are created every day. Use your imagination: You may establish the next reenacting society or horse club.

Breed Organizations: If you own a purebred, or are simply interested in one particular breed, existing groups and organizations can fuel and foster your interest. Much of the fun comes from breeding, but even if you are only interested in the riding aspect, breed-specific activities are available to you. At some breed shows, like those for Arabians and Paso Finos, riders dress in the traditional garb of the horse's country of origin. Those who own Chincoteague Ponies may find themselves devoted to saving their horses' wild counterparts.

Jousting: Many clubs still practice the art of medieval jousting. Riders use their horses (often draft horses, which most resemble the medieval war charger) and perform at Renaissance fairs. The focus is on the ancient sport itself as well as the elaborate turnout that accurate jousting requires.

Parade: Some organizations, like the Shriners and other service groups, have parade divisions which may use mounted members.

Reenacting: The reenacting of historical events enjoys enormous popularity, and many of the organizations that reenact history have mounted displays. If you are a history buff, consider joining one of these groups with your horse. You may find yourself riding with the cavalry. Reenactors seek historical accuracy, so part of the fun here is outfitting your horse with the period-appropriate gear.

Sidesaddle: While it is no longer considered scandalous for a woman to ride astride, sidesaddle used to be the only way for female riders to sit their horses. Today, many women still practice this skill, often in elaborate riding habits, and also compete in special sidesaddle events.

Societies: "Boutique" horse activities like carriage or sled driving often have their own societies that attract like-minded people with these interests. Some horsey clubs don't even require horse ownership: clubs that work to save wild horses or promote a certain breed or methodology, for example.

Getting Back Into Riding

For many of us, the love of horses and riding begins in childhood. You may have taken lessons as a child, ridden at summer camp, or even owned a beloved pony. School and other interests sometimes eclipse childrens' love of riding, but the desire to saddle up often reappears later in life. Renewing an interest in riding can be difficult. You may not be in the shape you were as a child, either physically or mentally. Children can be fearless riders, and adults are typically more cautious, with a better understanding of the dangers involved in being around horses.

But the love of riding persists, and it is a strong impetus for rejoining the riding community and renewing an old passion. You may not find things exactly as they were in your memories, but you can revisit the enjoyment you took from horses then. An experienced trainer, who has worked with adults before, will be helpful to you.

Selecting a Trainer

Even for people who have been riding for years, a good trainer can make all the difference in the world. Many trainers are geared toward showing. They can make a better living this way, with schooling fees, trailering fees, and lessons at the show. Also, many trainers spend enough time on the show circuit themselves that training similar-minded riders works well. If you don't show, however, you can still learn a lot from a trainer who does.

Having specific goals helps as you talk with a trainer. She can understand what you are looking to learn, and as she gets to know you and your horse, she will help you evaluate your progress and keep setting goals.

To find a trainer, word of mouth is often best. Talk to friends and fellow boarders at your barn. Take your

Your trainer should work well with both you and your horse.

time finding someone. You should observe a lesson given by your prospective trainer before taking one yourself. The trainer should invite you to a lesson for someone at the same level of riding you are—you don't want to watch someone schooling over crossrails if you are jumping 3'6", and at the same time, watching someone who is at a higher level than you can be intimidating. You want to get as clear a picture as possible of what your lessons will be like.

Notice basics—safety first. Your trainer should be

dressed appropriately, in heeled boots and long pants, with a helmet if she will be riding. Is the trainer on time? Is she focused on the lesson at hand? If the horse is hers, does he seem in good condition? Is he sour or bored? Is the equipment safe? Look for worn stirrup leathers, or ill-fitting tack. Is the ring safe, with good footing? A field can be a perfectly fine place to give lessons, as long as the footing is solid, and any possible hazards are marked or pointed out at the beginning of the lesson. If there is equipment like jumps or barrels, are these in decent condition as well? Is the fencing around the ring or field sound and safe?

Watch the lesson carefully. Does the trainer respond with praise when something good happens, or is she only focused on correction? Does she praise the horse as well as the rider? How does she demonstrate what she means? There are times when it is best for a trainer to climb aboard and show you what she is trying to describe, but some people prefer that their trainer teach through verbal instruction only. (Only you know your best learning style.) Does the trainer have the student go through a variety of exercises, or does she seem to be enacting a tired routine? How does the lesson end? Is there a summary of what happened, and instructions for what to work on next? Are the student's questions answered fully? Does the horse seem physically able to stand the work asked of him by the trainer? Does the trainer address her student's fears in a calm and rational manner?

If you like the lesson you watched, arrange to take a trial lesson next. Some trainers even offer this first one for free, but be prepared to pay her standard fee. If you will be using a horse belonging to your trainer or a school horse, allow a bit of extra time to get used to your new mount. During this lesson, make sure you ask any questions you may have, and pay attention. If things go well, and you want to return, you've found yourself a new trainer.

You may want to book "ground lessons" once in a while. Instead of riding in a ground lesson, you learn horsemanship skills. These present good opportunities to learn how to bandage a horse, how to load a horse into a trailer, even your trainer's favorite method for cleaning a stall. Ground lessons may also cost less than those addressing mounted work, but may not, as some trainers charge by the hour, regardless of purpose.

Dealing with Fear of Riding

Fear is a legitimate part of equestrian sports. Horses are unpredictable animals, and most riders have at least one accident forever emblazoned in their memories. There's an old saying that "Seven falls make the rider." This may or may not be true, but if you manage only seven falls while you're learning to ride, you're doing well.

Fear can get in the way of achieving your goals, so it is important to find ways to minimize your fears. Maximize your safety. Always dress properly for the sport you're doing—eventers should wear body protectors, and everyone should wear a ASTM/SEI-certified helmet (yes, even Western riders. They make them with cowboy hats over them, or you can wear one of the all-purpose ones.) Consider safety stirrups, too. If you don't like the way the "peacock" ones look (those are the stirrups with the rubber bands on the outside that many children use), there are plenty of safety stirrups on the market that don't reveal their true purpose. But safety stirrups will help if you should ever get dragged, and they may make you feel more confident as a result of their added security.

It may become clear that you are not in fact scared of riding, but of your horse. While this may lead to the painful decision to sell an animal you've become fond of, it may also make you excited about riding again. If you find yourself dreading mounting your horse, take a break from him. Borrow a friend's steady mount, or use school horses if you can. If you enjoy riding those horses but are still apprehensive about mounting your own, consider that you and your current horse may not be the perfect match. It's hard to have to sell a horse, but it's important to realize that it may be beneficial to both of you to find other partners.

Know your limitations, both physical and mental, both yours and your horse's. If you're out for a trail ride with three buddies, and you come to an open field, someone will almost inevitably say, "Do you want to canter?" If you don't, because your horse will run away with you (or because you are afraid he will), speak up. It is much better to deny your companions one canter through a field than to do something you're apprehensive about. Remember: Your horse can tell if you're nervous.

If you don't want to jump that ditch, or gallop across that field, he will know. Also, one bad experience can make a fear worse, where avoiding it and tackling it later, in a more reasoned fashion (such as cantering along a fence line with a trusted buddy instead of taking off across a meadow), will produce better results for both your confidence and your horse's.

If you're having a lot of trouble because of fear, consider consulting a sports psychologist who specializes in helping riders. These people make use of techniques like positive visualization and other strategies that can help alleviate fear and make you a more confident rider.

Stabling Your Horse

If you have enough acreage and the time to do it, you may keep your horses at home. For many of us, though, horsekeeping is not practical. This is where boarding stables come in. Paying to stable your horse means that you can own a horse without making the commitment to house and care for him yourself every day.

Where you board your horse can affect what kind of riding you do, as boarding facilities often attract riders with similar interests. You may even hear different places described as hunter-jumper barns, or dressage barns. Of course, some boarding stables house diverse groups of riders, with dressage riders practicing leg-yields as endurance riders head for the trails. But many follow the spirit of one discipline.

This may occur because of the trainer headquartered at the farm. Some trainers are associated with just one barn, and if that trainer teaches jumper riders, her students may board there. And that barn will therefore attract more jumper riders. A barn at which many trainers come in and give lessons may offer more variety in terms of discipline. As you look for a barn, talk to its boarders. Will you be the only one trying to get to shows on weekends? Or the only one who wants to ride the trails and keep them in good shape? It's often more pleasant to seek out a barn with boarders who have

Having other boarders to ride with is a benefit of boarding your horse.

similar interests to yours. On the other hand, you can learn a lot from boarding with people with different riding styles and different horses. Either way, where you board can affect what kind of riding you do. At the most basic level, an urban stable may not have trail access, but may allow you to ride more by being closer to your home. But the extra drive time can be worth it if you like to ride in fields and on trails, and if riding is one way you get out of the city.

Remember that the most important thing about a boarding facility is that it means you can ride. So if the pastures are so far from the barn that by the time you catch your horse and tack up, it's too dark to ride, it might not be the right place. Try the place down the road with lights in the outdoor arena, or spend more money for a place with an indoor arena. Consider the weather in your area, as well. If the winters are especially bitter, a barn with an indoor arena will provide you with more riding time.

Look for safety in a boarding facility. Fencing should be sound and strong (wood or electric, no barbed wire), and the stalls reasonably clean. Drop by unannounced at a barn you're considering at least once so you can see an "everyday" scene. Be sure you feel comfortable with the staff at a boarding stable you're considering. These are the people who will be around your horse, so watch as they lead others, feed, and do other barn chores. If you don't like how the horses are handled, that's a warning sign that you won't be comfortable leaving your own horse there. The manager should be someone you feel

you can talk to, since it is crucial for your horse's safety and your own peace of mind that you be able to discuss your concerns with the barn manager.

The other boarders are also an important part of any stable. Having people to ride with means more riding for those who don't like to ride alone. And you can tell quite a bit about a barn's "personality" from the boarders. Are people friendly when you come to tour the barn? Do they seem to be considerate of one another? Watch as they handle their horses and speak to each other. If people seem to be snippy with other boarders or rough

Sand rings offer a safe and contained place to school horses and practice skills like barrel racing.

with their horses, the barn may not be a pleasant place to spend time.

Examine the facility itself. Look at the rings. If you ride in the arenas often, make sure they are dragged and maintained enough to be safe and comfortable for you and your horse. What do the grooming spaces look like? The tack room? Fancier is not necessarily better, but even the humblest establishment should be reasonably clean and tidy, with a feed room horses can't get into and storage for saddles.

Ask about ring-use policies. Are you expected to move jumps in and out when you want to use them? If you take lessons, will there be other people in the arena when your trainer is there? Cost is always a concern, as boarding stables are very expensive to run, and often difficult to afford. (For more on keeping boarding costs down, see Chapter 6.) Are all the costs posted? You don't want to get a bill for blanketing if you believed it was included in your monthly fee.

Instead of boarding at a stable, you can keep your horse at a family farm, or a "backyard stable." You will not have the advantages of an on-call manager, or someone else managing your horse's worming schedule, but you may have more autonomy, and may also pay less.

Trust your instincts when it comes to selecting a boarding facility. A place that feels good to you, and where you can easily imagine yourself and your horse, will probably work out for you.

Schooling

Schooling, or ring work, is typically thought of as an exercise in getting ready to show. That's why it's called schooling—it is preparation for competition. Horse shows typically take place in rings, whether the competition is Western Pleasure or stadium jumping. Ring work can mean both flat work (anything not involving jumping), and jumping. It is practice and variety. Ring work includes riding patterns like figure eights, working on lateral movements for suppleness, and generally contributing to your horse being a better mover. Ring work is training.

Schooling is a discipline in and of itself. You do not have to be working toward a certain division or show to get a lot out of ring work, both for you and your horse. It is these patterns and practice that get your horse supple and balanced. Even a horse who never needs to learn to jump a course or ride a dressage test will be a better mount if he is in balance. A correctly ridden and conditioned horse is more resistant to injury than a horse who is schooled erratically or ridden out of balance.

Having Someone Else Show Your Horse

We're all familiar with the owners of racehorses getting their pictures taken with their horses in the winner's circle. Many everyday horsepeople are trainer and jockey as well as the owner. But if you are in a situation where you own a horse who you feel may benefit from being shown—or if you simply love horse shows but dislike riding in them—consider having someone else show your horse.

This is commonly your trainer. After all, she knows your horse very well, and can appropriately judge which classes he might do well in. She will also know what could be a challenge for your horse, and what goals he could achieve in the show ring that you might be able to work toward with your training. During your lessons, you might work towards a specific class, and she might ride him in that class.

She might also suggest that one of her other students show the horse for you. Depending on that person's level of skill and how comfortable you feel around her, this may be a winning situation for all. If you like to cheer your horse on more than guide him around courses, you may be able to give an eager competitor a chance to ride while you take pleasure in the work you have done.

As you set goals for yourself and your horse, keep an open mind as well as a desire to achieve those aims. When you accomplish one objective, set another. Keep moving forward, whether along established rungs of achievement or through a more radial pattern, learning different skills and different ways to enjoy your horse. Knowing yourself, your horse, and why you ride are all part of horsemanship.

Natural Horsemanship 2

Natural horsemanship has become very popular with equestrians in the past decade or so. Many different natural horsemanship practitioners have developed widely varying methods. Overall, though, natural horsemanship looks to the nature of horses as a basis for training. It represents what many horsepeople see as a much-needed shift away from equipment-oriented methods and punishment. If your horse feels too strong for you, for example, some traditional trainers would have you try a more corrective bit to ask the horse to respect your requests. A natural horsemanship clinician might have you do work in a round pen or on the ground to make him more

Many horses enjoy gentle handling techniques like laying an affectionate hand on the neck.

responsive. Of course, riding itself is not natural—horses' bodies were not made to carry people—but understanding horse behavior can help you take a more "natural" approach.

Incorporating natural horsemanship ideas into your riding and training does not exclude more traditional training. In fact, many of the ideas espoused by natural horsemanship clinicians are also important to conventional trainers, who may have been using them long before natural horsemanship became fashionable. So even though patience, for example, is an important part of natural horsemanship, it's also key to any mode of working with horses. The natural horsemanship movement has simply brought many of these ideas to the fore.

Some natural horsemanship techniques stem from old or even ancient methods like those ancient Greeks and Native Americans used to train their horses. The legend of the horse whisperer pervades natural horsemanship. The whisperer, myth has it, could understand and speak to horses with gentleness, and the idea of "whispering," and being gentle with your horse, has remained important to natural horsemanship training. Clinicians also cite cowboys or trick riders as inspirations.

Natural Horsemanship Practitioners

One of the assets and problems of natural horsemanship is that there are many different practitioners out there competing for riders' attention. These people are often featured in magazines and perform at horse expositions. They fill clinics and lecture halls, write books and host instructional videos. Each has a different approach, and system of instruction. Some focus on spiritual communication with horses, while others seek to bring techniques from non-Western cultures to contemporary horsemanship and riding.

It's fun to watch natural horsemanship demonstrations, and you can learn while the clinician puts star pupils or audience members through their paces. Often, the clinician will treat problem horses. You may see a rider with a horse in tow, telling the practitioner that the horse will not enter a trailer, or bucks people off. Then the clinician will "treat" the horse in front of the crowd, demonstrating how her or his methods can improve the horse's behavior. Some will also start horses in front of audiences, using a green horse from the community to demonstrate natural horsemanship skills in training. These demonstrations offer some of the most dramatic moments as you watch a formerly untrained horse accept a saddle and rider for the first time.

Many clinicians have certain tutorial systems, which include special products, books, and videotapes. You may find that you really like one person's style and equipment, but you may also see merits in many different ways of going about things. You may want the special or name brand gear, which can make things simpler if you're following one person's program. But you may also do well on your own, using some of the ideas you've gathered from different teachers. You may want to use your favorite clinician's books or videos to guide you further and give you some goals to work toward as well. Trust yourself. Sort out what you like and don't like.

While natural horsemanship teachers have widely varying techniques, there are some consistent tenets among most of their teachings. They may have trademarked names of saying these things, but for the most part, their methods emphasize understanding your horse and his behavior as a means toward better training. Comprehending how your horse perceives the world is an important part of natural horsemanship.

Thinking—and Feeling—Like a Horse

There are all kinds of excellent books on the specifics of horse behavior, many of which provide anthropological takes on various herds and breed mentality. But the most important key to understanding many natural horsemanship theories are the ways in which horses use their senses.

Horses hear very well, with their mobile and flexible ears. When you talk to a horse, he may not understand the words you use, but he understands your emotional state, whether you are confident or frightened. A horse will often only turn his head toward a strange noise, not his whole body. That position allows him to run away if he needs to. Horses hear far better than we do, so you can depend upon your horse having heard a strange noise before you have. When you're out trail riding, and your horse pauses and perks his ears, he might have already heard that bicycle or group of hikers, long before they come into your range of hearing or sight.

Horse eyesight is not as keen as human eyesight. The placement of their eyes on their heads does, however, allow horses much greater peripheral vision than we have. Their eyes work independently of one another, with a small overlap right in front. They also have a blind spot directly behind them, which is one reason never to approach a horse from behind, as they may kick out defensively before they realize it's you. Horses can see well in the dark, something you may have noticed when you're looking for your horse in a dark field and he approaches you first.

Horses have a keen sense of smell. They greet each other with their muzzles, and will recognize you by smell also. (Your horse may notice if you change shampoos or perfume.) When you see a horse with his upper lip flipped back, an action known as the Flehmen response, he is using his extra sense of smell within the membrane inside the lips. It's often seen during sexual interest, but horses will also do this when they encounter a new odor. The old saying that horses can smell fear is true in the sense that they do perceive the shift in scent that a frightened person emits.

Horses love to taste sweet and savory flavors. Most horses love molasses, and some like peppermints. Sugar cubes are a traditional hit. Carrots and apples are also popular, and probably the most healthy horse treats. Try feeding apples and carrots (cut up to reduce the risk of choking) in a feed pan on the ground. There are myriad commercial horse treats available, often molasses or peppermint flavored, and you can make your own with oat flour and molasses.

Horses' skin is so sensitive that they shake all over when a fly lands, and their whiskers help extend this acute sense of touch. When you trim your horse's whiskers, you reduce his ability to detect his surroundings. It's customary to keep them trimmed for shows, but it's considerate to let them grow if you're not preparing for competition. Horses will groom each other with their lips and a light touch with their teeth. Touch is also our primary mode of communication with our horses, from patting to how our legs communicate to them as we ride.

Horses talk, too. The nicker (that fluttering of nostrils accompanied by a soft snorting sound) is a greeting. Your horse may say hello to you with a nicker when you approach. A real snort from a horse can mean danger is coming, and a squeal is usually a sound made when the horse is upset or does not want to be approached. Horses give a loud neigh when they are announcing their presence. Another horse may neigh back so the two friends can locate each other.

As anyone who has watched a group in a pasture knows, horses have a strong herd instinct. Herd leaders eat and drink first, and they decide when the whole group should gallop across the field. If you want to prevent the

Once they are familiar with their handlers, many horses will respond to friendly hands on their noses.

flight reaction so innate to the horse, you have to be the leader of the herd. By overcoming the fear in yourself, you may be able to calm your horse down. Try this: if you're out riding, and your horse begins to snort and toss his head when he sees something unfamiliar, take a deep breath and let it out between your lips, making a horsey noise. You can transfer your relaxation (in the exhale) to him. Also, try talking to him. Although he can't understand English, he can certainly understand the calmness of your voice as you explain, "It's just a scarecrow, nothing major, you've seen them a million times before." Or sing. It's hard for either of you to stay too flurried during a chorus of "Old MacDonald," and singing forces you to breathe, which in turn makes you more relaxed.

Watching the Herd

To keep all the lines of communication between the two of you, spend time with your horse when you're not working. When he is turned out, go to his pasture and stand around. At first, you will be a big attraction, and he as well as his buddies may come over to sniff your pockets and see what kind of treats you have. But once it becomes clear you are not there to take any of them out of the field, they will probably meander off and go back to grazing, dozing, and playing.

Watch your horse. Who are his friends? Can you tell where he is in the herd? Does he have one special buddy?

Notice where he likes to eat, and how he approaches the other horses. If a truck drives by, does he spook, or barely even notice? What about bicycles, or airplanes flying overhead? Does he lie down at all? What do other horses do when they see yours coming? When you lead him out, does he pin his ears at certain horses? Do others pin their ears at him?

Try to find more than one day to spend in the pasture. You may feel silly standing out there at first, but watching your horse can help you get to know him better. The most easygoing horse will show you a side of his personality out in the field that he won't when you are riding him. You may see why he gets so herd-bound when

Even when he is grazing, your horse's behavior will offer clues to how he will behave under saddle.

you realize how bonded he is to a certain pasturemate. Or you might notice that the horse who seems so difficult to get along with is having some trouble fitting into the herd. You'll know to be extra cautious near bicycles if they always make him spook, or not to be overly stressed if you see deer if you've watched him graze near them. The pecking order you'll observe is very important to horses. Although it may seem like each horse should want to be at the top, that's more of a human ambition. It's usually more important for horses' security to know where they stand than to reach the top of the order. If your horse approaches other horses with his head low and humble, or is consistently waiting his turn at the trough or round bale, he may be fairly far down.

Unless his herd rank presents a health or safety problem (like he is dropping weight because no one will let him near the hay), it's fine that he is not an alpha horse. And next time you are trying in vain to get him to take the front position in a ring game of follow the leader, you will know why he is having trouble and be able to work with him on his own terms. The point is to understand where your horse is in relation to his pasturemates, because finding out if he's a lone wolf or likes to run things can help you with your riding. A very dominant horse, for example, may be difficult to keep at the back of a group trail ride. You can then decide if you want to try to change this behavior under saddle, or simply offer to lead the next time you are out in a group.

Bonding, Patience, and Other Natural Horsemanship Tenets

There are many exercises you can read about in natural horsemanship books to relate to your horse on the ground. Some of the most basic include having your horse follow you in an arena, an activity which some believe signifies that your horse trusts you. Many horses will follow their owners around off the lead rope unbidden, for a few steps at first. They key is not to look back at him and to keep walking. If you realize after a while that he is not following (you cease to hear the tell-tale hoofbeats), you can decide if you use the lead rope for a few steps before trying again.

As your horse begins to follow you around, try walking patterns of figure eights, circles, and around jumps or barrels. Stop, change direction, and pick up speed at will. Your horse will follow you around, and you can test this newfound bond by making tighter and tighter circles as well as walking more intricate patterns around the ring. Don't try this in an open field, as the chance that something will spook your horse is too great. In a ring or paddock (a ring is best, since there is no grazing opportunity, but a paddock will work too), make sure the gate is closed and start walking.

Eventually, your horse may even follow you over jumps. Don't set them high, or you won't be able to take them yourself. (You might want to try this by yourself the first time, since the sight of you hurdling the oxer in the ring, especially if your horse won't follow you at first and is watching you curiously from a distance, is not something your barnmates are likely to forget.) But be very careful—you really do have to pick up some speed to jump ahead of a trotting horse.

Besides the bond between horse and person, another tenet of natural horsemanship is patience. For example, you may allot an hour to coax your horse into a trailer. And he may load right in the first time, so that you've only spent a minute on a task you'd rationed an hour for. But he may also take even longer than that. If you try every gentle approach, and let him take his time, chances are he will eventually load. But it could take far longer than the hour you've set aside.

If something in your training is not working, natural horsemanship dictates that you need to slow down and look at what you're doing. Should you be jumping this horse at all? Is he really balanced enough to take off and land in rhythm? Or are you not ready to jump as high as you'd like, so you're perching forward or leaning back or otherwise hindering his progress? Don't rush. You may need an educated opinion, or you may need to spend some time riding another horse to see what it is "supposed" to feel like, or you may need to spend some time strengthening your horse physically and mentally. Trying to do things within natural horsemanship parameters often seems very slow. You need to be patient and above all, flexible.

As the parent of any young child knows, flexibility is what keeps you from going totally insane when you're dealing with another person's needs, feelings, and even

mood. You may decide it's the perfect day for a long, lazy trail ride. But your horse is in a bad mood, and picks the same day to try you at every turn, by halting, jigging (prancing rapidly and nervously), and rearing. You can work through all of this with patience and time, but you also have to realize that your dream of the peaceful trail ride has been replaced with a training session. The rest of the party may have to leave you behind as you ask your horse to walk in quiet circles until he is responding enough to behave on the trail.

With natural horsemanship, you work at the horse's pace, which can be frustrating and very slow. Natural horsemanship intends to teach the horse at his pace, not on your schedule. This also means that you stop whenever you get the reaction you were seeking, even if you've

Playing and interacting with your horse is a great way to get to know him better.

only been working for a few minutes, a technique recommended by the Greek cavalry master Xenophon as well as more current natural horsemanship trainers. This can be tough when you've scheduled an hour with your horse into a busy week, and he actually does what you want early on in your ride. Then you may have to shift your plans from a working session to an easier hour of conditioning or trail work.

Stop asking your horse to do something once you have a positive response. In the case of the frustrating trail horse, as soon as you have him moving deliberately forward, walk on for a little while but then head for home. You may have wanted to stay out longer, but your horse will associate the idea of getting to quit and go home with his decision to follow your requests. The horse who achieved your requests so early on can get another challenge, or be turned out with you watching his behavior at liberty. As Xenophon wrote, "It is the best part of lessons if the horse gets a season of repose whenever he has behaved to his rider's satisfaction."

Flexibility also comes with the understanding that what to do often depends upon the situation. A very young horse who jigs on the trail may be frightened or just wondering what's going on. But your formerly easygoing ten-year-old trail horse who starts jigging may have a new physical problem or be getting sour. Each situation and horse is different, and you need to approach each one with renewed innovation so you deal with the problem as it affects your horse and situation.

Always have a plan. It may not be the plan you

would have selected, but you should still have a course of action. If your horse starts shying at a tarp laid near the arena on a windy day, work through it. Ask him to approach slowly, and if he keeps shying, consider getting off and leading him closer and closer. Don't risk becoming frustrated and angry with your horse, which can only erode your relationship. If you're not making any progress, or he's becoming increasingly frightened, consider turning him back out for the day. You can always try again later.

Sometimes you'll hit a dead end. Your horse, who was jumping 2'6" fine, is suddenly refusing or otherwise having trouble. It's very easy to get frustrated and angry or to give up. But if you can remain calm, and put the jumps down to crossrails, you may find he regains his willingness to jump. Then you can try with the jumps set a little higher until you are back where you wanted to be. The key is to go back to the easier job before your horse gets too upset to go forward at all. Restore his confidence, then worry about moving on.

Mindfulness and Natural Horsemanship

Remember to use your mind to train your horse. In a physical contest, as any rider knows, he will win every time. By planning all sorts of different challenges within the parameters of any given exercise, you out-think your horse and therefore maintain a leadership position. Don't just ride aimlessly around the ring, but point him toward a certain fence post. Leg yield him as you ride a long fence line. Longe him for ten minutes one day before you ride, and the next week afterward. Keep asking for different things or he will get bored and sour.

Horses will get bored by any activity within about ten minutes. Providing the change that keeps them from getting sour does not have to be too elaborate. You can keep changing direction and locations in which you work. Even if your barn has a terrific arena, once in a while, take your horse out in the pasture to ride or even to longe him. A "trail ride" can be as simple as a walk around the farm, both ways, or even along the fence line.

Natural horsemanship includes a willingness to backtrack. Much of natural horsemanship goes with the idea of getting very comfortable at one thing before trying another, more difficult exercise. Anyone who has spent time in the jumper ring knows how this works: you start over crossrails, and keep moving up. A horse who starts refusing at one height may work through it if you go back to his previous height and show him how easy it is instead of forcing him over the larger jump. The same principle applies to the natural horsemanship process. If you're working on having your horse respond to a tiny bit of pressure, for example, you may need to start using a bit more before he "hears" just your fingertips asking him to step over or back. Again, patience is key.

This also means you have to know your horse. An experienced rider recognizes the squirrely feeling that an unsure horse gets on the way to a large or new fence. Sometimes she can provide the confidence for both of them, but sometimes the horse clearly says, "I'm not going over that." Then the attuned rider can make a circle, take something lower, or otherwise deal with the situation. Once you have been working with your horse for a while, you will know when he is getting uncomfortable. Watch for physical signs like fidgeting or repeated balking. An uncomfortable horse may also arch his neck, carry his head very high, or perk his ears far forward.

Imagination helps a great deal in natural horsemanship (and with anything involving working with horses), since there may not be one specific alternative to try. Get creative. Say your horse won't walk over the heavy board you've designated as a trail obstacle. You have tried and tried, but he shies and turns away. You don't want to give up, because what you're asking is reasonable and within his capabilities. Consider this: what will he walk over? A tree branch? Your jacket on the ground? A line you've drawn in the arena sand? Keep thinking and asking your horse to walk over these things. Eventually, he may become so confident in his ability to walk over things that he will step across the original board without flinching.

The Round Pen

The round pen provides a place to improve relations with your horse from the ground. It teaches the horse to focus on you and what you are asking. "Round pen work" often means free longeing, or longeing without a longe line, although it can also be simply asking your horse to lower

Work in the round pen is one of the primary natural horsemanship activities.

his head, or turn in a circle. Having the horse trot around the pen while you're in the middle is a common round pen exercise. When he tries to slow down or come in toward you, you flick the lead rope at him and make him keep going until you ask him to come to you by lowering the rope. Some take issue with this, saying that it is just another mechanism of fear, but other clinicians use it with impunity, with the idea that it teaches the horse that you are in charge, and can be trusted. Decide what you are comfortable with, and what works for your horse.

Many natural horsemanship clinicians depend upon a round pen as the optimum space in which to work with a horse. If, however, you don't have access to a round pen, you can still do natural horsemanship work. In a field, an arena, or even in your horse's paddock are all acceptable places to practice some of the activities you and your horse have learned.

Riding Bareback

Bareback riding used to be a circus trick. But bareback riding is also a terrific (and "natural") way to ride. Bareback riding helps you develop an understanding of how your horse's muscles work, and become attuned to his way of going. Bareback riding helps you be a better rider with your saddle as well—you'll be amazed at the security of seat you can develop from riding without a saddle, especially at gaits like the sitting trot, which can be difficult to maintain with fluidity.

You can ride bareback at the walk from your earliest lessons, but save the trotting and cantering for when you've become a bit more experienced. Don't grip too tightly on the horse's side to keep your balance, since he'll just respond to the pressure by scooting forward and possibly unseating you. Instead, try to maintain your usual good riding position, and let your legs hang gently. If you're having trouble riding "naked" (horses can be very slippery), you can use a bareback pad. This is a saddle-shaped pad with stirrups. It's a step between riding bareback and having a full saddle. Another helpful tool is a neck strap, which you can grab if you need to rebalance yourself. You can just use a stirrup leather, buckled loosely around your horse's neck for this purpose. You can always use your horse's mane for this purpose as well; try anything to avoid snatching your horse in the mouth if you lose your balance.

Natural Horsemanship Clinics

If you do get interested in natural horsemanship, chances are that you will find yourself at a clinic. In the horse world, a clinic is a few days devoted to learning from one teacher, an opportunity to learn directly from the person behind the books and videos. Some clinics also allow time for one-on-one lessons, usually at an extra cost to you. Many natural horsemanship practitioners—and many other horse professionals, from dressage teachers to team roping specialists—spread their lessons through giving clinics. Often over a weekend, students will bring their horses to a central barn that is hosting the clinic. The days will include group lessons given by the clinician, and often lectures as well. There may also be auditors, who pay to watch the lessons but don't ride in them.

People who have studied under the most famous clinicians often have their own clinics. These, which are usually far less crowded, can be as beneficial than gaining audience with one of the big names. These trainers have mastered many of the same skills (the biggest clinicians have their own ranking and seniority systems for their students) but will not charge as much or create as much of a furor with their presence as their teachers will.

If you have a favorite natural horsemanship practitioner, hosting can be very worthwhile to find a way to bring him or her to you. Find a clinician who will appeal to the people who will be attending. Check with those who have been to the clinician's clinics before (online is a great way to do this), and check to see what your putative classmates want. Clinics can be expensive, so be sure the students you have lined up are enthusiastic about the event and the person giving it.

Give the clinician you select plenty of advance notice—up to six months or a year for the very busy or famous ones, and less time for their disciples. You may be dealing with her office during these initial contacts, when you describe your facility and what you're looking for as well as hearing what they expect. You don't want to assemble a group made up of half children only to find that the clinician only works with adults. Find out what the clinician requires as well. Will you need to arrange a ride from the airport? Where will the clinician stay? Where will she eat? Many have standard agreements, but if the person with whom you are dealing does not, you will have to draw up your own agreements.

Spend some time figuring out how much the clinic will cost, so you can give your classmates some idea of what they will be spending. Be sure to advertise your clinic, with invitations or simple posters around various local horsey sites.

Consider charging auditors, because it just tends to make everyone take things more seriously if they've paid. It's a good way to help defray costs. And auditing is a great way for you to see a clinician whom you may or may not want for your own clinic later.

Horse Communicators

Slightly on the fringe of the natural horsemanship world, but nevertheless benefitting from its popularity, are the animal and horse communicators. These people, who often take more literally the tradition of the whisperer, claim to be able to talk with horses and understand them. Their services are not for the skeptical, but many horsepeople use them to find out what their horses may be thinking, and the practice is more common than many imagine.

Horse communicators, or horse psychics, suggest that people and animals get to know one another better through telepathic and intuitive communication. They often are called in to help solve behavioral and health situations, and may even try to contact dead horses for their bereaved owners. Much psychic or telepathic work with horses has come from those trying to figure out the reasons for reoccurring behavioral problems or issues. Some work alongside veterinarians or farriers to help determine the horse's take on his situation. And some animal communicators will even work by telephone.

Equine Massage

Just as many people do, many horses benefit from massage. Learning to give equine massage is another way horse owners communicate with their animals. There are various techniques and branches of equine massage.

There are massage styles that focus on the motion used on the horse's body, and others that use massage as a post-workout treat for the horse.

Anyone can reward a tired horse with a nice, hard rubdown with a towel, but deeper tissue equine massage needs expert guidance. You can hurt your horse if you go about it the wrong way. There are books and instructional videos available, and some equine massage therapists hold clinics as well. Some equine massage therapists work on saddle fitting, concentrating on how the horse carries his saddle and rider as a means of understanding his way of going and any problems he may have under saddle.

Aromatherapy is another of the non-medical avenues available to people seeking natural healing for their horses, and can be used in conjunction with massage. Some think that applying essential oils to a horse's body can help him alleviate certain problems, like fidgeting or general jitteriness. (Conversely, many people find the aroma of horses therapeutic.)

Aromatherapy uses the acuteness of horses' sense of smell to soothe or inspire them with favorite odors. Oils of lavender and chamomile have been reported to quiet horses, just as they are supposed to relax humans. Just be careful that your horse does not have an allergic reaction to anything you are applying to his skin, and that he can't find the oils and accidentally ingest them.

• • •

Natural horsemanship is not a strictly delineated endeavor. Between its numerous practitioners and styles,

Work over cavaletti improves your horse's confidence and your security.

there are many ways to apply natural horsemanship's teachings. And many of the concepts intrinsic to natural horsemanship reside in the teachings of more traditional trainers as well. But what all these practices have in common is a willingness to consider ideas outside the parameters of tradition as well as those within. In that respect, natural horsemanship can help us all become more imaginative riders and horsepeople.

3

Handling **Horses** and Riding **Etiquette**

Riding is the way most of us spend the most time with our horses. We often get interested in the sport of riding first, and then fall in love with the horses themselves. But horsemanship requires time on the ground as well, teaching your horse how to act when you're not mounted, and training him with longe lines or long reins. General handling also includes how your horse leads, and helps make him easier to work with. If his ground manners are good, chances are his behavior under saddle shows the same effort.

Ground manners extend beyond how your horse behaves to how you behave around the barn. The ancient sport of riding has its own etiquette, much of which is derived from the horsemanship goal of staying safe. How you treat your horse and others when you're dismounted reflects upon your achievement as a horseman. Common—or "horse"—sense prevails.

Grooming

Grooming gives you time to look over your horse as well as clean him.

Grooming, the process of cleaning a horse and getting him ready to ride, is the beginning of any work on the ground. Although some people have their horses groomed and tacked up for them, grooming is an

important skill to develop. Not only are you preparing your horse for the ride ahead, you're also spending time with him. Even though you typically groom your horse before you ride him, sometimes it's pleasant to give him a full grooming even when you're not riding. It's a good time to speak calmly to your horse, and treat him with the same kindness and firmness that you will demonstrate once you're mounted.

Grooming is essential before you saddle and bridle a horse, because it keeps irritating dirt from getting trapped in between the leather and the horse's hide. You can examine him for any injuries as you groom him, and also assess his mood. Show grooming requires another level of preparation, often including extra steps such as braiding a mane and tail and polishing hooves, but everyday grooming can be done fairly expeditiously. Even on days when you're not competing, good grooming shows respect for your horse and sport.

Make sure your horse is securely tied before you start grooming him. You'll need both hands free as you work. Be careful as you go so that you don't apply too much pressure to anywhere sensitive. You'll learn your horse's sensitive spots as you groom him. He'll pull away or flinch if you touch somewhere ticklish, and may let his lower lip droop in pleasure if you find one of the places he likes to be scratched. Don't overgroom a pasture-kept horse in the wintertime, because some of the natural oils in his coat keep him warm and dry. Manes and tails should be picked free of burrs with your hands. Avoid combing either of these, because you'll pull out hair. If you like, you can use the dandy brush lightly on the mane, and a commercial detangler to prevent burrs from sticking or to add shine.

Keep your grooming supplies in a clean container, like a tote box or wooden tack box. Clean and disinfect them every month or so by dipping them in a bucket of water with about a cup of bleach, then laying them in the sun to dry. Don't borrow or lend brushes, as infection can be passed through grooming supplies. Below are a few of the most basic tools for grooming, and how and when they are used.

Body Brush: A soft brush that takes off the finer layer of dirt, it's also used in the direction the hair grows, and adds shine once you've done the heavier cleaning with the currycomb and dandy brush.

Currycomb: This is a stiff rubber or plastic tool (they used to be made of metal, but these are too harsh to use on a horse) that helps to loosen caked mud, and other tough dirt. You use a currycomb in a circular motion. Keep the currycomb away from legs and face, because the skin is too thin in these areas to tolerate something that hard.

Hoofpick: This is a pick, typically made of metal, that lets you clean the horse's hooves. Some have plastic handles and a stiff brush on one end to clear away dirt. Go from heel to toe so that you don't hurt his frog accidentally, and while you're down there, check his shoes.

Sponge: A small, damp sponge is useful for cleaning around your horse's eyes. Another sponge can be used to clean his dock (the area underneath the tail), and around his sheath.

Stiff Brush: After currying your horse, you use a stiff, or dandy, brush to remove dirt and brush it away. These are good for long coats, and are used in the direction the hair grows. As it gets dirty, brushing it against the currycomb will lift dirt.

Towel: This comes in handy for wiping the horse's eyes, and removing saddle and girth marks when you rub him down after a ride. Never put your horse away with girth marks still on him. It also can be used after the soft brush to make his coat shinier.

Bathing

In the summer (or even in the winter if you have access to warm water and a heated area), you may want to bathe your horse. He can be in cross-ties in a wash stall, which has a hose and a drain, or tied with a quick-release knot to something near a hose.

There are many commercial horse shampoos and conditioners on the market that you can use, or you can use mild dishwashing liquid. Any soap will be diluted in a bucket of water until you have a bucket of suds. Conditioners are applied after washing.

A large sponge (the type you use for washing a car) is very helpful as you wash your horse. Rinsing is key, because left-over soap can irritate his skin. Pay special attention to his mane and tail, which can be difficult to rinse. Also be careful as you wash his face, because getting soap in a horse's eyes will sting and make him more difficult to bathe in the future. Many horses dislike having hoses near their ears, so turn yours to a trickle when you wash his head. You may find a stepstool useful as you do this.

If your horse is to be turned out after his bath, consider either toweling him off or hand-grazing him until he dries. Horses tend to roll after being bathed, and if he's still wet when he rolls, all your work could turn to mud.

Ground Manners

"Ground manners" is the equestrian phrase for how your horse behaves when handling him on the ground. A horse with good ground manners is easy to lead, loads into a trailer, stands quietly when he's being tacked up, groomed, tied, or clipped, and doesn't bite or kick.

When you lead your horse, always use a lead rope. Traditionally, you lead from the horse's left side, but your horse should be accustomed to leading from either side, so that he does not become agitated if you ever need to lead him from the right. Lead him with one hand near the halter, and with the other holding the folded end of the rope. Don't drag him by his halter, no matter how gentle he is. If something does scare him, you could get dragged or your hand snapped back. Don't make a coil with the free end of the lead rope, either, because it can tighten dangerously around your hand. If your lead rope has a chain, avoid gripping it so you don't hurt your hand.

Be careful when leading your horse into small spaces, like cross-ties or a stall. He can't pivot as easily as you can, so he needs some space to turn around. Whenever you turn him out into a pasture, he should be facing the gate you came through (locked when you came back in). This way he is less likely to buck and run off to join his friends, and possibly injure you.

Many barns have cross-ties, which are ties, installed across from each other, suspended from the walls. You clip a horse's halter into these, and they are very convenient, as they secure him easily. (Cross-ties should have a piece of twine, called a safety string, between the tie and the metal loop affixing it to the wall so that if a horse is scared, it will break and free him.) There are also panic snaps, hardware that serves the same function. But there are always times when there won't be cross-ties available and you'll need to tie your horse up.

The most basic thing about tying a horse is that it needs to be done with a quick-release knot, which allows you to undo the knot quickly by pulling on one end. Have someone show you how to do this, and then practice until you are comfortable with it. Don't ever tie a horse by the bridle, because he can easily snap the reins with one jerk as he glances over his shoulder to see who is whinnying at him. If you need to tie him once he is tacked up, use a halter and lead rope over the bridle. Ideally, your halter should either be leather or, if it's nylon, at least have a leather crownpiece. Some nylon halters also now come with breakaway pieces. An all-nylon halter will not break if the horse panics and rears back, and he could flip over.

Make sure that you're tying your horse to something secure, like a hitching post or tree. Tie him at about back level, because if the lead rope is too low he could trip over it. If he's tied too high, he'll be straining his neck as he stands.

Patient training makes for quiet loading and easier travel.

Longeing

Longeing and long reining are two varieties of dismounted schooling, also known as "work in hand." In longeing, the horse circles you on what is essentially a very long line. In long reining, there are two long reins with which you guide your horse from behind him.

Longeing a horse is a training exercise, and is not as easy as it looks. You will be amazed how much effort it takes to longe a horse in an even and steady manner. How well longeing works also depends upon how used your horse is to it. He may have been longed plenty before you got him, in which case he can help you learn. If longeing is new to him, however, you may need some help if you are not familiar with it yourself. Consider booking one lesson before you longe your horse, as you can hurt him (or yourself) if things go awry.

A horse being longed typically has a surcingle and side reins, which help keep him in the proper position—or "frame"—as he works. You can see his progress and how he looks when he's moving in a way you cannot from his back. Some people will longe a fresh horse without this gear just to wear him out a little before mounting, but usually, longeing is used as a training method. It's also great exercise for him on days that you cannot ride. Just remember that since longeing is harder on your horse than riding (working on a small circle is stressful to his joints), don't do it for too long. Twenty minutes is plenty.

Be sure your footing is level. Stay out of his range

Learning to longe with proper equipment, like side reins, will pay off in balance and pacing.

of kicking (especially if you're longeing a fresh horse), and use galloping boots on his front legs if he has a tendency to nick himself. Always change directions frequently, to avoid straining one side.

When long lining, you essentially have two very long lines that are not attached to each other. It is done without side reins, and is sort of a transition between longeing and riding. In long lining, you either stay well behind the horse, and work with him from the rear

(imagine a person plowing), or stand to the side, more as you would with a longe line.

Once you get to advanced long lining, there are many ways to adjust the lines to maximize the horse's work on flexion and control. If you (or your horse) haven't worked with long lines before, you will do better with help from a professional.

Long lining in a straight line helps a horse to respond to direction given through rein contact.

At the Boarding Stable

If you have your horses at your own barn, you can keep things as you like them and indulge your own preferences.

You can let your dogs run free, and leave your tack in the center of the aisle if you like. But at a boarding stable, you have to submit to more order, so that things can run smoothly. Given different riders and views on how things should work, boarding barns are fraught with possible trouble. They're a bit like college dorms. Everyone needs to pitch in and work to get along to make things run smoothly. They also can have a club aspect, since people often have the same sports interests. Boarding offers you built-in riding buddies, but being a boarder can also require some finesse.

To help things keep working well, show general consideration for the management and the facility itself. Pay your board bill on time. Although their purpose is often recreation, boarding facilities are still businesses, and it's important to respect the management by keeping up with your financial responsibilities. Since the board bills are what keep the barn going, late ones can be detrimental to the horses' upkeep. When you're late, you are potentially harming everyone's horses by delaying improvements that are waiting for funding. In drastic situations, barn managers or owners may need to place a lien on a horse whose owner is tardy with payment.

Do your part to keep the barn clean. Shovel or sweep up manure your horse leaves in the aisles right away, and if the barn is small, put your grooming supplies away when you're finished with them, even if this means you'll need to fetch them again after you've ridden. If you see that your horse has broken a fence board or other item around the barn, say so. Usually these accidents are just part of upkeep for the farm and the management, but candor is always best.

Be thoughtful toward your fellow boarders. Always ask before you borrow something from another boarder or the staff, even a squirt of fly spray or a hoofpick. Others' tack, and certainly their horses, should be considered entirely off-limits unless you have express permission to borrow them. Show consideration by not leaving your horse in the cross-ties while you're doing something else, keeping your area of the tack room or your locker reasonably neat, and following general safety rules. You may feel sure that your aged and peacefully grazing horse is not going to run away, and drop his lead rope. But if he does spook, he could hurt other people as well as himself, by scaring nearby horses with riders, or causing an accident with a car. At a boarding barn, your decisions affect more than you and your horse. Gates require extra care. Each time you lead your horse out of the pasture, ask yourself if you locked the pasture gate behind you securely. If you left the farm on a trail ride, did you lock those gates behind you as well? Even if your horse is not an escape artist, someone else's might be, and disaster could result.

Look out for each other. If you get your horse from the field, and notice a bloody gash on one of the other boarders' horses, notify the barn staff. It may be a fresh wound that needs veterinary attention. Boarders can be each other's greatest assets in an emergency, since they provide a constant rotation of people in and out of the field.

It can be tricky being helpful without being nosy—what looks like a bad scrape to you may have already been treated by the horse's owner. You may rush in with the hurt horse, leaving your own in the pasture, and find his owner is in the barn. She tells you that the vet has just been there, and said to wash the wound and turn the horse back out. You may feel silly upon hearing that the horse has already been treated, but when animals' welfare is at stake, it's better to be extra cautious. If the wound really looks that bad, no one will blame you for your actions.

However, you don't want to seem as if you're criticizing anyone's mode of horsekeeping. In the case of a true emergency or animal abuse, you should act swiftly and without worrying about the owner's feelings. But in more questionable cases, sometimes the best course of action is to take your concerns to the barn manager. Horsekeeping is much like child-rearing in that people are very touchy about others' interpretations of their actions, and criticizing others (especially behind their backs) leads to tension in the barn.

This care with words also applies to the management. You may have questions or concerns about how your horse is being treated by someone on the staff. Instead of taking these problems to your fellow boarders, take them directly to the manager. If you tell a fellow boarder you feel like your horse's bucket is never quite clean, you may start a rash of complaints, as well as a reputation as a complainer. But if you quietly tell the manager, she will probably take care of your horse's bucket right away, and start looking more carefully at everyone else's.

Try to be considerate of the barn manager. Don't bother her unnecessarily, or call her when you can't find your martingale. If she lives on the farm, respect her privacy, and don't bother her at home unless it's an emergency. Just as she should be very clear about what you can expect from her, you should be very clear about what she can expect from you. If you know your farrier only comes to your barn between 9 and 5, and you work during those hours, you know she'll always have to get your horse in to be shod and turn him back out. You wouldn't want her to wait until the last minute to call you at work and say she wouldn't bring the horse in, so give her advance notice. If special fees need to be worked out, you can discuss them before the situation arises. The more courtesy you show her, the more under-standing she will demonstrate when you and your horse need special favors or help.

Visiting a Barn

Being a guest at a boarding barn is just like being a guest anywhere else in that you should be gracious and unob-trusive to your host. In this situation, your host is more than just the friend whom you're visiting. Instead, you're a guest of all the boarders at the barn. Use common sense, erring on the side of caution. When you are at a friend's barn, you may see some things that are not done as they are at your barn. Unless you see something unsafe, it is generally best to keep these criticisms to yourself.

Try not to disrupt the routine. Leave your dog at home. Watch where you park, making sure not to block any path that barn staff may use for the tractor or manure spreader, or that other boarders need to use. If you have your trailer with you, ask where to park it. Be sure that your horse behaves, and don't leave him in the cross-ties or wash stall unattended. Don't pat other people's horses, or offer them treats—you never know what kind of diet the horse is on, and would hate to offer him something he was allergic to. Also, some people simply don't hand-feed their horses, and if you do, you could undermine their training.

When a friend is visiting your barn, stay with her, and help her follow the rules of your barn. If she will be riding, make sure she signs any release forms your barn may have.

Ring Manners

Riding in a ring also requires manners. If you have ever watched people schooling before a show, you have seen the ultimate exercise in this, as riders weave in and out of each other, going over jumps and constantly changing direction. But even in your home riding arena, you need to pay attention and be courteous to the other riders.

The "rules of the ring" include passing left shoulder

to left shoulder when you are coming toward another horse. If you're coming up behind someone, say "outside" or "inside" so they know which way you're coming. (Inside is generally best unless the other horse is far off the rail.) The main idea is not to cut someone else off, which is dangerous as well as irritating.

Watch your speed as well. If you are walking while others are trotting or cantering along, it is polite to stay off the rail so they don't have to navigate around you. If you're the one riding at the higher speed, don't bear down on walkers from behind. Always beware of the most novice rider in the ring, who may not be used to riding around other horses.

If you're jumping, let the other riders know what you're doing. Call out the names of the jumps you plan to take. Saying "Flowerbox to oxer," allows people time to stay out of your way. If you change courses, say so, and when someone lets you know the jumps they are aiming for, pay attention, and don't be trotting a small circle right where they should be landing. Try not to ride through the middle of a lesson (although the reverse is also true: a lesson should not mean others cannot ride unless this is a barn rule).

Trail Riding

Trail riding manners concern both the riders you may be trail riding with and the environment you encounter when you leave your own farm. You should always make sure that you are on a trail on which horses are permitted. These may be bridle paths at state parks, or local easements and fields. Know your route. Will you be on clearly marked paths? Carry a map with you if you're in an unfamiliar area. If a farmer is permitting you to ride in her fields, stay to the outside and do as little damage as possible—don't let your horses trample the corn. Also be very sure to close all gates, so that any livestock turned out cannot escape.

Trail riding alone is dangerous because if an accident happens far from home, you will be stranded without help. If you do head out by yourself, carry a cell phone with you. Although there are special holders for these to go on saddles, carry yours on a belt holder or otherwise on your own body. If you and your horse become separated, you don't want him to be the one with the phone. Also, leave word with someone at the barn when you've left and when you expect to return, so that if something does happen, someone will know to come looking for you. If no one is around when you depart, leave a note or notify a family member so that someone knows you are out on the trail.

Group trail riding has its own set of manners, some of which come from foxhunting tradition. These stem from the fact that riding in a group can be dangerous, so some systems are in order. Horses tend to get very excited when they're all together and may behave more like a herd than a group of mounts. So everyone needs to be on her best riding behavior when out on the trail with others.

Trail rides should move at the level of the least experienced rider, because the horses will tend to follow one another. If you take off cantering across a field, it will be difficult for the novice in the back to control her horse. If it will really be burdensome for the more advanced riders in the group to maintain a slower pace, the group can split in two.

Even though riding with more advanced riders often helps your own riding, it's also bad manners to accept an invitation with people who will be doing many things you're not yet comfortable with, like jumping

Give other boarders' horses a once-over glance as you get yours from the field. Check for wounds and lameness.

logs or fording streams. You'll hold people back, and will also be more at risk than those used to these obstacles. Better to go with one or two trusted friends who can help you navigate new terrain before you head out. The same goes for your horse. You should only take a proven mount on a trail ride. It's unfair to the other riders to use a trail ride as a training session for your young or unproven horse. Again, start out with people who are going with you for the purpose of helping with a training session for your horse.

Wait for each other on the trail. Don't head out until everyone is mounted, and don't leave a stream until all the horses have had a chance to drink. Unless you're out riding your own property, leave your dog behind. You'll be too busy riding and enjoying the day to be a responsible dog owner, and other people in your group or using the trail may not appreciate having your dog along.

In a large group, having a "trail boss" and a "drag rider" (who rides at the back of the group) is helpful. These people can make decisions and help the less experienced members of the group. One of these leaders should have a first aid kit, and a replacement boot in case a horse loses a shoe along the way.

As you ride, don't ride right up on the person in front of you—at least one horse length is the rule of thumb. Only ride abreast when there's enough room.

A red ribbon in the tail signifies a kicking horse, so if you see one, stay well clear, and if your horse kicks, use a red ribbon. Let the other riders know what you are going to do. If you want to pass the person in front of you, say so. Use hand signals, as you would driving a car, to indicate if you are speeding up or slowing down to the person behind you. Don't hold branches back, as well-intentioned as this is, because they can hit the person behind you. The foxhunting term for danger, which is used by many trail riders, is "Ware" (as in "beware"). So calling out "ware branch" warns your fellow riders to watch out for a low-lying branch.

Consideration for others who use the trail keeps them open to horses, so be mindful of those who will follow you. Pick up all the garbage you leave if you stop to picnic. "Pack it in, pack it out" is the rule on most bridle paths. Now that mountain biking and hiking are so popular, many trails formerly devoted to horseback riding are multi-use. This means everyone has to work to get along, since the sports are so different. Technically, the cyclists should yield to hikers, and everyone should yield to the horses, but this may not happen. To stay safe, use the right side of the trail as you would on a road. Uphill traffic has the right of way, so if you're heading down, move to the side to let cyclists pedal past.

Remember that many other trail users have not been exposed to horses. Be courteous when that cyclist rides up too close behind you and spooks your horse, or that hiker with the loose dogs and children makes you pull over and stop your ride until she has everyone under control. If you can muster politeness, you might remind them about the dangers of being around horses. You may want to put a small bell on your horse (if he'll tolerate it) to warn others of your presence. But in general, and especially with cyclists, you have to be on the alert. Keep your eyes and ears open, and watch your horse. He'll hear a bike long before you do, and you'll notice his ears pricking toward it. You may wish to pull over instead of having a discussion about who has the right of way. Your primary concern is keeping yourself and your horse safe.

To help your horse not spook, talk to other trail users in a friendly tone. If you greet a cyclist or hiker, and they respond verbally, your horse will know that they are people. Otherwise, the strange gear and noises may make your horse think he is encountering an entirely new (and terrifying) creature, when all you see is a man with a backpack. Also, friendliness is good public relations for the equestrian community. With more and more trails becoming multi-use, we need all the help we can get.

Keep to a walk or trot on the trail. Cantering and galloping are better saved for the fields and rings at home, because the uncertainty of the trail can cause an accident if someone on a recumbent bike comes cruising around the corner just as your horse is finding his pace. It's easier to stop suddenly if you maintain a slower pace.

Try to avoid riding on pavement when you can, as it's hard on a horse's hooves and carries the additional danger of cars. Sometimes, however, you will have to cross a road or ride along one for a little while. Keep to the right, but don't ride in ditches. Let your horse stop and look at an approaching car if he seems fidgety, and if you need to, hold out your arm so that drivers see you are asking them to slow down or stop. Always hop off if you feel unsure—there is no harm in walking alongside your horse instead of on him if it makes you more comfortable. Always run up your stirrups and bring your reins over your horse's head as you lead him.

Ground work and etiquette may seem like what you have to get through in order to enjoy riding. But it provides a foundation for your time in the saddle as well. Even your behavior toward other riders on the ground forms a basis for your work as a horseman, as you demonstrate respect for your sport, your horse, and your fellow riders.

Basic **Veterinary** Care | 4

You don't need to be a large animal veterinarian to own a horse, but you do need to know when to call one. It's important to understand equine wellness so that you can keep your horse healthy. The key to handling many situations yourself is knowing your horse and having the confidence to handle his minor health problems. Then you'll be able to establish when your horse is feeling well, when you can take care of his problems on your own, and when to call the vet.

Conformation

The chestnut on the left appears straight in front, a benefit for any breed or discipline, while the dark bay in the center has the leggier look preferred by many who ride English. The stocky chestnut on the right has the deep chest favored by many Western riders and breeders.

There are many times you will need to evaluate a horse. When you're checking out options for a ride, or out shopping for a horse, it is good to know a bit about conformation. Conformation means how the horse's body is put together. If a horse has good conformation, his body is predisposed to make him both comfortable to ride and likely to stay sound.

A horse with good conformation has limbs that are clean, without old injuries or deformities, and symmetrical, so he can move without hurting his joints. His head is in proportion to the rest of his body. He has a deep chest, strong hindquarters, and a gracefully long neck. Viewed from the front, his hind legs are directly behind his forelegs. His body seems level from his neck back; a horse's rear end should not rise above his withers. His legs are straight and properly set, neither too close together nor too far apart. He's usually more handsome than a horse with poor conformation.

Obviously, looks are not the most important thing when it comes to horses, and many characteristics often deemed unpleasing—like lop ears or an eye that shows a lot of white—have no bearing on the horse's usefulness. Except in halter classes, pretty is as pretty does. Breeding can affect what is perceived as attractive; a Quarter Horse connoisseur might not appreciate the dished face that makes an Arabian breeder proud. You can ask a breed expert or read breed literature to find out which features are most desirable in particular breeds.

Most horses do not have perfect conformation, and which shortcomings you can live with varies widely depending on what you expect the horse to do. In general, conformation affects soundness. Conformational defects are more than aesthetic drawbacks; they prevent the horse's weight from being evenly supported, which in turns puts stress on certain areas. Simply put, a horse with poor conformation is more likely to go lame than one with good conformation.

You may want to avoid purchasing a horse whose conformation defects can lead to unsoundness. Toeing in—when a horse's toes point toward each other instead of straight ahead—is a good example of a defect that isn't technically an unsoundness, but can lead to it. A horse who toes in can be more apt to develop splints (hard lumps that develop between the splint and cannon bones) or ringbone (bony lumps on the pastern bones). That doesn't mean that a horse who toes in is unridable, just that he is predisposed to become that way. He may never go lame, or he may start having trouble the day you get him home. These factors explain why you need to have a pre-purchase exam. Your veterinarian's evaluation will help you decide what to do.

The Pre-Purchase Exam

Your relationship with your horse's veterinarian begins before you own the horse, because your vet should do a pre-purchase exam, or vet check, on any horse you are considering buying. It's best to have your own vet do the exam. If the seller offers to have her vet do it, politely say that you'd prefer yours, as you don't want a conflict of interest. (Her vet may, however, have potentially useful information about the horse's history, and can be a valuable resource.)

A pre-purchase exam should check your potential new horse for soundness and evaluate general health. Make sure you discuss everything that concerns you with your vet during a pre-purchase exam; she will be able to advise you if you're looking at a potential hunt partner or a lawn ornament. Vet checks do cost money, so it's tempting to skip them if you like a horse. Nevertheless, you should always have one. Ultimately, a vet check can save you a lot of money if it helps you avoid an unhealthy or unsound horse.

Keep in mind that the veterinarian's check provides an evaluation of the horse on the day he's being seen. You may also get extra testing, like radiographs. But don't expect the vet to tell you whether or not to buy the horse, or how much you should pay. Those are decisions you will make on your own with the information you glean from the vet check.

At the exam, the veterinarian will palpate (feel) the

The vet will ask you to jog the horse in hand during a pre-purchase exam so that she can evaluate his gaits and check for lameness.

horse's body, checking for old injuries and other imperfections. As she feels the horse's legs, she will be checking for healed-over injuries or other unsoundnesses that could affect the horse's way of going. She will examine each foot and hoof for conditions like founder or windpuffs, and general swelling. She'll flex each joint, and use hoof testers to check each hoof for sensitivity.

Then it's time to watch the horse move. Your vet may ask the horse's handler—who can be you or a helper—to spin the horse in a circle so she can see if he appears to have any neurological problems, and to jog him toward and away from her so she can see any lamenesses or irregularities in stride. In a flexion test, the vet flexes the limb to exert pressure on the joint. She then releases and has the handler jog the horse off to see how the joints fare under duress.

Many vets will next ask that the horse be ridden so that they can evaluate him for the job he's supposed to do. You may want to ride the horse, or you can ask the seller to do so. It's best to be in a place with various surfaces, so the vet can see how the horse reacts to different footing. She can then evaluate his comfort at all his gaits. This bit of exertion after being ridden will enable her to check him for respiratory problems as well.

There are a few follow-up tests the vet may recommend. If there is any reason to suspect that the horse is drugged, she may want to do a blood screen. Some leg problems show up best on an ultrasound, and some joint problems are most visible on radiograph. These tests may be suggested to give you an even clearer picture of the horse you want to buy.

The vet check will usually uncover something. Then it's up to you to decide if you can live with whatever that something is. If a horse is sound at the vet check, you may decide to live with an old bowed tendon. You may do the same thing if he has arthritis that no longer seems a problem. But be very cautious before purchasing a horse that has foundered or is navicular. These conditions heavily predispose a horse toward lameness and can be harbingers of more costly medical care. If the veterinarian discovers a serious condition, think carefully before taking on a horse who may sadly prove to be more of a patient than a mount.

Bringing the New Horse Home

Besides the pre-purchase exam, your new horse needs a Coggins test test for EIA (Equine Infectious Anemia), since you will need that vital piece of information if you show him or travel anywhere with him. A copy of the results should also stay on file at your barn. The new horse will need any outstanding inoculations. He should have his teeth checked and his feet done by a farrier. Then he should be isolated for a time. Ask your veterinarian how long, since this time can vary depending on locale. Start a record book for him, and deworm him at least a day before turning him out in your pastures. Horses pick up different parasites from different pastures, and you want the horses you already have to be protected as well as your new one.

Horse Wellness

The best way to avoid large vet bills and general anxiety from a sick or hurt horse is to keep him well in the first place. Obviously, this is not easy, since accidents and illness will happen. But you can save yourself some time and trouble by concentrating on getting to know your horse and how he looks and behaves when he is feeling well.

A healthy horse is in good weight, neither skinny nor too fat. His normal temperature is between 99.0 and 100.5 degrees Farenheit, and his pulse is 30-50 beats in a minute. You find the pulse by putting your fingertips on the artery on the edge of the lower jaw (under his chin, almost to the throatlatch), and count beats. (It takes some time to find the pulse, but once you do, you won't lose it again.) The tail is shiny and active, held straight in the center. His droppings form balls that break on impact. His ears are alert, following you around. The healthy horse's eyes are bright without discharge, and there is a salmon-colored membrane around the eye. His nostrils won't flare while he is at rest, and his skin should be supple. If you pick up a fold and release it, the skin should smooth right out again (if it stays up, the horse may be dehydrated.) His coat is smooth and shining. He'll take weight on all four feet, although he may rest one of the back ones. Horses like to eat, and a healthy one will be trying to graze and eating his hay.

Every time you go to get your horse, look him over for anything unusual. You'll develop your own system for checking him. One way is to look from the feet up. Another method is to look at the horse's hind end on each side, the front end in the same manner, and then, of course, his head. Any way that works for you is fine. Just include every section in your appraisal, and be consistent. Try to look at him the same way every time, so you learn to count on your own evaluation.

Check your horse's shoes. Has he pulled one? Has he stepped on it in such a way as to twist and reset it? Are the nails getting loose? How long are his toes? Look for cracks, flaking, and caught stones. If the nails seem loose, ride gently for the day, and call your farrier. (It helps to make each shoeing appointment at the time of the last one, so you know the farrier will be there in four to six weeks regardless of whether your horse throws a shoe before then.) If your horse's hoofs look cracked, it may not be anything to worry about if he has "shelly" or white, soft feet. If cracks are unusual for him, consider painting his feet with a hoof moisturizer. If your horse has overly soft feet, there are hoof growers and hardeners you can use. If your horse's hoofs seem mushy, or smell "rotten," he may have thrush, which can be treated with a bleach solution or a commercial preparation.

When you look at his legs, check for swelling, heat, and cuts. Run your hands down each leg to help detect these problems. All four legs should be uniform, without

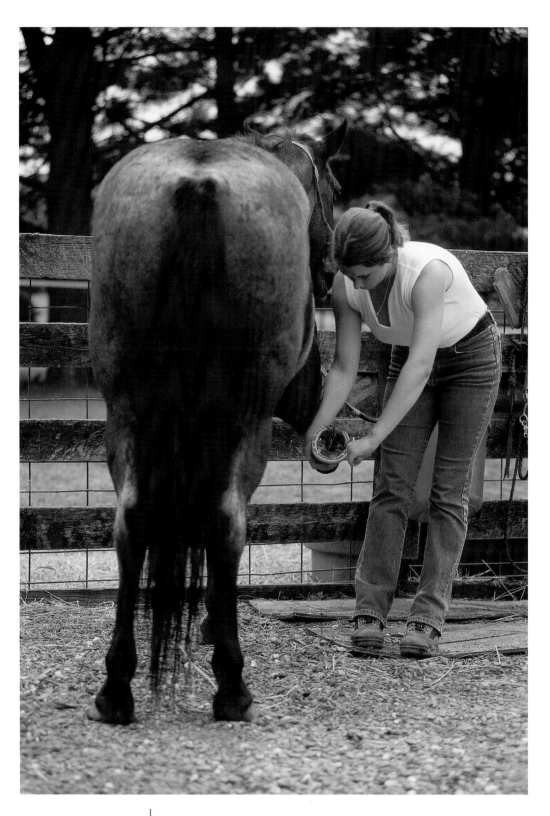

bumps or heat. Look for swollen joints like knees. (Any of these difficulties may have shown up in a lameness as you brought him in.) It takes some time to develop the ability to detect lameness by listening to footfalls, but you can easily see if your horse is favoring one leg or the other.

As you begin to survey his body, looking along his shoulders and topline, look for contusions. You can doctor any minor scrape with some topical antibiotic ointment. Anything that appears deep or does not stop bleeding means you should call the vet. Continue looking at his body and coat, checking both sides, and his hind end.

Then move up to the head and neck. (This all seems like it will take a long time, but you get very speedy at it.) Look at the eyes and make sure they are clear and not seepy. This is especially important during fly season, when horses are prone to eye infections. Look at his nostrils. Some clear mucus is all right, but if there is some odiferous discharge from his nose, he could have a sinus infection. Check his mouth as you put in the bit. If he is holding his mouth awkwardly, or trying to avoid the bit, he may have a tooth problem.

Keep a first-aid kit ready in your barn so you can treat minor wounds. The kit should have cotton, a stretchy gauze wrap, vetwrap, non-stick dressings, adhesive tape, bandage scissors, bottled water for cleaning wounds, an iodine solution, wound dressing, healing ointment, petroleum jelly, leg bandages, and liniment. A miniature version of the kit is a good thing to take on

Opposite page: Picking out your horse's feet provides an opportunity to examine his hoof health.

It's important to have basic leg bandages on hand and to know how to apply them. Ask an experienced person to show you how to wrap legs properly.

a long trail ride and keep another in your truck or trailer.

Learn to handle medicines safely in case your horse needs treatment. Your vet will give you detailed instruction when she prescribes the medicine, including how to give medicine by mouth and by intramuscular injection. Be sure to tell your vet about any other medications your horse has had recently. Much horse medicine needs to be refrigerated and like human medicine tends to lose its effectiveness over time. Throw old medicines away.

When To Call the Vet

Your horse should get a checkup at least once a year, and you should aim to develop a relationship with your veterinarian. You want your veterinarian to be someone you trust, and can reach when you have concerns. This can be hard to do, especially if your horse is at a boarding facility, where the manager may handle veterinary visits, but it is worth a try.

Even if you handle your own worming and basic shots, you should get to know your veterinarian as preparation for more serious situations. For example, if your horse will not eat or seems badly hurt call your vet. It is often more dangerous to believe you know enough not to "bother" your vet. While we all hate to be the sort of person who calls the vet each time a horse gets a scrape in the field, it is truly better to err on the side of caution than to risk your horse's well-being. If your vet does not agree, question your choice of practitioner.

Some vets may want you to take your horse's temperature rectally (remember to tie a string on the thermometer so the horse does not "swallow" it.) Have all your information in order before you call the vet. And write down the symptoms you have noticed and any questions you want to ask. Most important, be there when the vet arrives.

If your horse exhibits any of the following symptoms, call the vet. Diarrhea, hard manure balls, or a runny nose (especially with yellow or green fluid), are all reasons for concern. Always call the vet if your horse is standing with his front legs out in front of him, refusing to move, because that means he may have foundered.

If he is pawing a lot and looking at his stomach, or rolling from side to side, he may be colicking. That technically means he has a stomachache. Get him up, and see if you can trot him on a lunge line, since sometimes exercise will expel a bubble. Since horses cannot vomit, colic can be very serious. Call the vet if you think your horse has colic, and while she is on the way, walk him slowly so he can't lie down and roll, which could possibly twist his intestines.

Sometimes your horse may just not seem right to you. If he's listless or seems uninterested in things that would usually cause him to look and listen, you might want to take his temperature. If he has a very high fever, your vet may ask you to try to bring it down while she is on the way. High fevers are rare in horses, but are also very serious. To cool a fevered horse, soak his neck and chest with cool water or cool, wet towels until his body feels less hot. You'll need to keep taking his temperature every fifteen minutes to see if you're making any progress.

You need to call the vet if your horse has gotten into the feed room and eaten his fill of grain. Too much grain can cause health problems from toxemia to founder, so your horse may need to have his stomach tubed with mineral oil. A horse who has gorged himself on grain requires attention within eight hours, but should be fine if tubed soon enough to arrest the toxins in the grain. If your vet is held up, she may ask you to stand your horse in buckets of ice water in case of possible laminitis as a result of the grain.

If your horse cuts himself badly, you should have the following information handy when you call the vet: exactly what part is cut (as in pastern or hock), how deep (describe the cut in detail), what the blood looks like (squirting or dribbling). Find out if he is lame from the cut. To dress the cut, wash it with an antiseptic soap, scrubbing with as much energy as your horse will allow, and then rinse it well. You can use a saline solution of ½ tablespoon per quart of water. Next, apply a non-stick pad, and bandage the wound to keep it clean as you wait for the vet. (Keeping your horse's tetanus shots current will help you relax if he cuts himself.)

Remember, you know your horse best. If something seems wrong to you, trust your instincts. Don't leave a horse suffering from an unexplained condition for more than a day. And never leave a horse in even a little bit of pain without knowing why he is hurting.

Prevention of Disease

Just as your constant attention can help a small injury or problem from getting worse, there are precautions you can take to help your horse avoid communicable diseases such as the flu or strangles. Horses are most likely to get these when they are around a lot of new horses in places like a horse show or even on a bridle path on the first warm day of spring. To minimize his risk, be sure your

A horse who has been on stall rest will appreciate some hand-grazing.

horse is up to date with all his vaccines. Try not to let him touch noses with strange horses you meet. And don't share buckets with other horses or let your horse drink from a public trough. Bring a clean bucket along when you take your horse out trail riding or to a show, so that you can give him his own water. Equipment, especially bits, can also harbor germs, so don't share them.

Once a sick horse is in the barn, take precautions to protect the other horses. Try to keep him away from the others. Don't use his buckets or even stall cleaning equipment for other horses. Use paper towels and rubber gloves when you're tending him. In fact, it's best if just one person cares for him, but if you have to care for him and other horses, do the others first. Then change your boots, or disinfect them by walking through a pan of disinfectant. (Rubber boots work best for this.) Wash your hands often. Disinfect his gear constantly. Keep taking the other horses' temperatures so you know if one of them has a fever, which could be a sign of infection. And try to keep traffic down as much as possible, so people are not carrying germs back to their own barns and infecting new groups of horses.

Helping the Vet

Once the vet comes to examine and treat your horse, you need to be able to help her do her job. That is, your horse needs to be still for treatment. Often you can just distract the horse by holding him. Scratch or pat him, and cover an eye so he won't see a needle coming. You can grip the loose skin at the shoulder, or even hold an ear to distract and calm him.

If your vet needs a horse to stand still, you can hold up one foreleg. Just stand on the same side as the vet. You can also use a chain-end lead shank as a restraint. Make sure the halter fits well, and run the chain end over the nose. Be very careful with this, since you can hurt the horse's nose if you are too severe. Your vet may want to use a twitch, which is something tight (a chain or a rope) around the horse's upper lip. The pressure releases endorphins that calm the horse and keep him quiet for a short period. Don't use a twitch for more than twenty or so minutes.

Worms

Worms lay eggs in the horse's intestines. Then, the horse excretes the worms' eggs along with manure. Next, the eggs hatch in the pasture, and then the horses eat the larvae when they're grazing. Then the cycle starts all over again. Each worm has its own specialty; some hurt the digestive tract, and others damage the blood system and other organs. Your veterinarian can test your horse's manure to see what kind of worms he has, and recommend a worming schedule that works.

If you do the worming, keep a schedule so you know which preparation you're using when, and be punctual about giving your horse his wormer. If you use a paste or a gel, give it to him before you give him anything to eat. His mouth may taste strange after you've given him the wormer, so he may not accept a treat from you even if you want to demonstrate your appreciation for his cooperation. One helpful thing to do is keep his head up after you've given him the wormer so that he doesn't spit it out. You may also want to stroke his neck with a downward motion to encourage him to swallow the wormer. Many wormers will dissolve eventually, so he will get the benefit of the medication if you can hang in there and coax it down.

If your horse starts looking really thin, worms could be a problem. Worms (really "internal parasites") can cause all kinds of internal damage and can harm or even kill your horse, so you want to get him on a worming schedule. You can worm your horse or let your vet do it.

Some larger boarding facilities like to keep all their horses on the same schedule, so you may simply get a bill whenever your horse gets wormed. There are all kinds of wormers and schedules, some of which depend upon things like the age of your horse and where you live. You should consult your vet about what schedule and which wormers are best for your horse.

You can reduce the likeliness of worms on your pastures by rotating the pastures and by making sure your horses are on a worming schedule. Try not to overpopulate the pastures. Also try to pick up manure, since keeping paddocks and pastures as clean as possible really helps keep worm populations down. On larger farms, dragging the field with a harrow can help break up manure piles as well. Try not to overgraze and overcrowd pastures, since the more horses per field, the greater the parasite population. If you can help it, don't distribute feed on the ground. Don't spread horse manure on horse pastures because larvae are hardy and can survive this process. New horses should have a fecal test for worms before getting turned out with other horses.

Equine Dentistry

Many vets will do dentistry work, particularly the "floating" (or rasping) of teeth that most horses need annually. (You should have your horse's teeth checked every six months, though.) If your horse needs special dental work, you will need to consult an equine dentist.

You should call the vet or dentist if your horse drops a lot of feed, seems to resist the bit, or seems to lose weight, because any of these can be tooth problems.

A horse does not lose all his baby teeth and have all his full-grown teeth, or a "full mouth," until he's about five. Horses' teeth grow throughout their lives. At the same time, they are always being worn down by constant use. The evolving changes in the appearance are what makes it possible to tell a horse's age.

If Your Horse Gets Sick

It's tough to handle an animal's illnesses, since it's up to you to detect what is wrong. Your horse depends on you to decide if he needs medical help. But with the help of a good veterinarian, you can handle many of his everyday diseases.

For one thing, keep good records. You should keep track of all your horse's checkups, and keep a datebook of when he is due to be wormed, shod, and given immunizations. Whenever you need to call the vet, write down the symptoms that have made you make the call in the first place. You should also know what time of year your horse is due for his Coggins.

Sometimes shots have to be given on a yearly basis, and sometimes more often if "boosters" are required. Your vet will tell you which is which. Basic shots you can expect your horse to get include tetanus, sleeping sickness (equine encephalomyelitis,) flu, and rabies. Depending on where you are, your horse may need Potomac fever shots, or shots for strangles or leptospirosis.

If your horse does get sick, try to be a good nurse. Make sure he has plenty of clean bedding to lie on, and stick to some kind of routine. A rhythm to the day will make him feel better by occupying him. Keep grooming him, and spend as much time with him as you can. Taking care of your horse while he is sick allows you to see if he's getting better or not. It can actually be a bonding experience for the two of you as well. Do whatever the vet asks you to do. If a dressing has to be changed daily, or medicine administered every eight hours, follow instructions.

If Your Horse Goes Lame

Don't worry as much about deciding which part of the leg is lame as much as whether he is lame. It can be difficult to tell that your horse is lame, and doubly difficult to tell where the lameness is. Trying to figure lameness out constitutes a major pastime in stable yards. You'll find people draped over the fence of the ring, watching a friend jog a lame horse. "It's in the stifle! It's that stifle acting up again!" one person will say, only to have the owner turn and say, "Did you all see that? It's definitely in the shoulder."

It's usually best to leave this kind of diagnosis up to the vet. You need to be able to tell if your horse is lame in the first place. To figure this out, jog him. This means you run alongside him as he trots. Keep the lead loose enough that he can move his head, and then jog in a straight line. A lame horse will favor his painful leg, which means he will try not to bear too much weight on it. Also, the sore leg will step with a more abbreviated stride, and if the lameness is in the hind end, your horse may throw his head down as the sore leg touches down. If the lameness is in front, your horse will throw his head up as his sore leg touches down. Remember: head down if the lameness is in the rear, head up if it is in front.

Check his feet first, because he may just have a stone in his shoe that he's trying to avoid. You can tell if something like that has happened recently by seeing if the frog of the hoof is puffy or inflamed-feeling. Feel his other feet to see if they (or any legs) are hot or swollen. This will give you a point of comparison.

Nutrition

The range of what a horse eats is vast. A horse's diets is determined by what he is used for as well as his age and size. Factors that can influence daily feed are condition, physical type, temperament, appetite, health, keeping, work, and weather. A broodmare's needs, for example, are very different from those of a stall-kept show pony, which again diverge greatly from those of a senior citizen out to pasture. And in the wintertime, pasture-kept horses will need more energy to weather the cold. So the first thing to do when figuring out what to feed your horse is to consult your veterinarian. She will help you draw up a plan that will fit your horse both in body and use.

The basic nutrients a horse needs are water, carbohydrates, proteins, fats, vitamins, and minerals. Many horses can get all they need from grass or hay, as well as a salt and mineral block out in the field. If your horse is in light to medium work and out to pasture, you may not need any supplements at all. If he's in light work (up to an hour a day of walking and trotting) your horse can get about 15 percent concentrates (grain or pellets). For medium work (some cantering and jumping), the ration goes up to about 30 percent, and for heavy work (competition and training), a horse gets up to 45 percent concentrates. Check with your vet. If she recommends a supplement, follow directions carefully.

Hay, which constitutes the bulk of the equine diet, must be high-quality. Higher quality hay is not just more attractive, it's also more nutritious. Look for hay with a green color, fine stems and leafiness. This indicates early-cut hay. Hay that's been cut too late is woody, and not as leafy. It's also not as nutritious. Watch out for moldy hay, which can make horses sick. Moldy hay is grayish (sometimes even with very gray or white patches) and has a distinctive odor. Once you've smelled it, you never forget it. If you have never seen it, ask someone to show it to you.

Grain (or pelleted feeds) need to be fed if your horse requires extra energy. A massive range of these higher-energy foods, from oats and barley to complex pelleted feeds, is available. Check with your vet to determine which suits your horse. Many barns use sweet feed, which is grain that has a touch of molasses added. The molasses makes sure the horses will eat it (horses love molasses) and also makes it less dusty.

You estimate a horse's weight with a special tape measure made for that purpose, or you can use an ordinary tape measure. His weight equals his heart girth (just behind the withers) in inches squared, times his length in inches, and divided by 330. Once you've figured all this out, write it down, and if your horse is boarded, make sure the barn manager has a copy. You'll be constantly tweaking the formula, changing it if your horse gets sick or if you change his work schedule. Make feeding changes gradually to allow the horse's digestive system to adjust. Don't feed your horse right after you ride. Because the blood supply increases during work the supply to the digestive system decreases, which could cause faulty digestion and colic.

Giving hay on the floor of his stall lets a horse eat naturally, as if he were grazing, but it's also wasteful. A horse with any kind of breathing problem should be fed this way, however, since it allows mucus to drain out of the respiratory system. You can put a bucket with grain in a tire so he won't tip it over.

Treats are another important part of feeding a horse. Although many owners give their horses treats out of hand, this makes some horses nippy. You'll have to judge for yourself if you feel comfortable hand-feeding treats to your horse. There are myriad commercial horse treats available, often molasses or peppermint flavored. Try feeding apples and carrots (cut up to reduce the risk of choking) in a feed pan on the ground.

All horses need fresh, clean water. Do not believe the old tale about water after feed being harmful. Unless he is very hot from exertion, in which case he should still be allowed measured amounts of water, a horse should always have an unlimited supply of water available.

Horse health care can seem very complex since new treatments and advances in veterinary medicine happen every day. For most horse owners, however, a good veterinarian, preventative care and a focus on wellness will help you give your horse every advantage.

Economical **Horse Ownership**

5

Horse ownership can get really expensive. Between buying your horse and caring for him properly, you will be paying vet bills, feed bills, and board bills if he is boarded. If he's at home, you can count on paying for bedding, barn maintenance, and possibly barn help as well. Add in riding equipment and training fees, and you begin to realize you have chosen one of the higher-priced passions around. If you have limited funds, but are still determined to own your own horse, there are ways to approach the situation to keep expenses down while enjoying your horse and being a responsible owner. Just keep in mind that the cheapest part of horse ownership is actually buying the horse. It's the upkeep that can make it so costly.

Remember, too, that buying a horse is a real financial commitment. You may get a great deal on a horse, and even find reasonable accommodations for him, but there is never a guarantee that the horse will not cost you a lot of money. For instance, a horse can have an everyday pasture accident, resulting in a leg injury. Then he will require costly veterinary attention, supplies, and a stall to rest in when you'd planned on leaving him out. You will need to pay the vet and your boarding barn for the higher stall board. Then, the day he is deemed sound to ride, he steps on the reins of your brand-new bridle right before his annual barrage of shots. Now you find yourself replacing a bridle as well as bracing for a yearly expense that you knew was coming, but did not know would be following such an immense financial outlay.

There are plenty of ways to lower the cost of riding and having horses, but everyone who loves and owns horses understands that expenses hide in every corner, and that there is always the possibility of a big bill. Horses depend on us. Buying a horse is not like buying a motorcycle or bike. It is more akin to having a contract with him that you will care for him as long as you own him and not just regard him as something to ride.

On a less serious note, horse ownership is extraordinarily rewarding. And shopping for a horse is fun too. Not only is the end result—a new horse—something you've been looking forward to and a wonderful finale, but the process itself is often both enjoyable and educational. You get to look at and ride a wide variety of horses. Also, you learn more and more about what you want as well as what you can live with. And there are a few ways to keep the price of your new acquisition down.

Acquiring the Less-Expensive Horse

For starters, keep an open mind. If you decide you simply have to have a tall, chestnut mare, you're bound to be disappointed when that stocky gray gelding turns out to be the perfect partner. Also, as much as you can, ignore fashion. Lots of white on a horse is very desirable these days. But those stockings and blazes could also elevate the price of an otherwise not-too-special horse who should be a bargain. An old saying goes: "One white foot, buy him. Two white feet, try him. Three white feet, put him in a dray. Four white feet, give him away." Now, with white markings in style, the saying would be just the reverse. The lesson is: don't pay too much attention to style and color.

One key part of finding a less-expensive horse is realizing that there will be something "wrong" with him. If he were flawless, he would not be cheap. Of course, he will seem perfect to you! But he may have qualities that render him less desirable to his present owner and possibly cause him to fall short of more objective standards. Blemishes, conformation faults, and breed deviations can all make a perfectly sound and usable horse cost less.

Blemishes (as opposed to unsoundnesses) are imperfections that may mar a horse's appearance, but do not make him less able to be ridden. A scar is a blemish; a bowed tendon is an unsoundness. A blemish can bring the price down, but beware of anything that will make the horse more likely to be lame. You may end up "paying" by not being able to ride. At the pre-purchase exam, your veterinarian will help you determine whether or not you can live with your potential horse's imperfections which is a key part of any horse buying venture, and is discussed at more length in Chapter 4.

Don't be too put off by conformation faults, such as a wide base (when the horse's legs are planted far apart in front). Much of the importance of conformation stems from what you want the horse to do. It's why Thoroughbreds, with their ground-covering gait, are some of the best horses to ride at speed, and why many Arabians, bred to last in hostile climates, make endurance champions. But remember too that it has much to do with how he's ridden, and his (and your) attitude.

Another way to save on a new horse is to use him outside of his usual reach. In other words, don't discredit a horse because of his breed. If you're not planning on doing breed showing, you can sometimes find a bargain on a horse who does not meet his breed's specifications but is still a great horse, like a Paint, who may be solid in color, and thus not entirely desirable for someone who wants to show him in Paint shows. Your undersized Percheron may not have the optimal strength his breed typically uses to pull heavy loads, but could turn out to be your favorite hunter. Also, smaller adults should not

rule out larger ponies, which can often be less expensive than their taller counterparts. Any horse who stands under 14.2 hands is generally said to be a pony, and as such is typically shown by children in pony divisions. But this does not make him any less an appropriate mount for the rider who can fit him.

Consider an older horse as well. A horse may have served his time as a show horse or even as a school horse, and be ready to move on to a new home. If you need a horse to trail ride and will treat him fairly gently, the older horse may be perfect for you. Often, owners of these horses do have to sell them because they can't afford the upkeep on both their older horse and their

From retired show horses to youngsters starting out, most horses appreciate time spent riding in the fields.

new one. But they want to make sure their old mount has a good home after all his years of work. If you can provide that home, you may not have to spend too much money.

On the flip side, very green horses can also be bought more cheaply than their "made," or well-trained counterparts. If you are an experienced rider, you may be able to find a very nice horse who has had little training. You may prefer this since the training on the horse will be your own. Just be sure you know your limitations, because riding a horse without enough training for your level of riding can easily result in one or both of you getting hurt. It may seem like you can learn together, but actually, horse and rider partnerships are often more successful if one of the duo has some good experience. If you're a green rider, you do not need a green horse.

Where to Look

Sometimes the best horses are only for sale through word of mouth. Your trainer tells you about a student she has who is selling her old dressage horse, or you know a senior in high school who will sell her horse before she heads to college. But for those times when you don't know where to begin, there are other, if better traveled, avenues.

Look at the bulletin board at your local tack shop, feed store, or co-op. These places, especially local ones,.are often clearinghouses for horses and horse services. It never hurts to ask the people who work at these places, either. They deal with horse people all day, and may know of exactly the kind of horse you're looking for. And if you're looking to save some money, you want to buy your horse locally.

Many areas also have horse dealers, or "sale barns." These are usually large establishments, devoted to buying and selling horses. These sorts of places often get a bad reputation from disgruntled buyers, and are often unfairly maligned. On the other hand, be careful when dealing with a sale barn. Often, the horses have not been at the barn long enough for the person who is selling them to know them very well, and sometimes the horses at a big sale barn are there because they are otherwise unsellable. They may be unsound, or have bad habits that make them difficult to keep. Take a trusted professional with you, and have your own vet do the pre-purchase exam.

Like sale barns, auctions can offer real bargains if you know what to look for. Try to stick to established auctions. These advertise well ahead of the sale date, and often provide printed catalogs. The auctions that crop up weekly or monthly often feature very troubled horses who have been starved or otherwise mistreated. Some wonderful horses are available at these sales, often sadly called "killer sales," since some of the prime customers are buying horses to sell for slaughter. But they're not for the faint of heart, and can lead to even more heartbreak if the horse you believe you've rescued turns out to be unusable or even moribund. If you have professional help and a good eye, though, these auctions can yield some good results.

At the scheduled and reputable auctions, you can find nice horses of all ages and descriptions. Many auctions' catalogs detail the horse's breeding, and will have a short blurb about him. Arriving well before the auction starts gives you some time to approach the sellers (called "consignors" in auction lingo), see the horse ridden, and ride him yourself.

There will often be a veterinarian on hand to do pre-purchase exams; however, if you are uncomfortable with having a vet you don't know do this for you, you will have to either take your vet along or see if the horse's owner will allow him to come home with you for a little while. Many owners will not do this, though, so don't be surprised if this suggestion is rebuffed. Also, seek out local sellers if possible. It's an added bonus to know the person you're buying from at least by word of mouth.

Auctions can be useful even if you're not quite ready to buy. You will see many people noting the price of each horse as he's sold, which is a way of gauging local prices. It's not a bad idea to do this in your own catalog, just to give yourself some rough idea of what you can expect to spend for the kind of horse you want.

Classified ads can really help. Look in the back of national horse magazines for ads, and check your local paper and any local horse publications. There are Internet sites with horse classifieds on them as well. Some particularly equestrian areas even have entire magazines devoted to horse ads. Classified horse ads have their own lexicon, so if you're confused by what the ad means, or have other questions, contact the owner. Here are some terms you might see:

action: motion of the horse—mostly in how much the legs flex. "Lots of knee action" can be a good thing for a gaited horse, like a Saddlebred, or a bad thing for a hunter.

amateur: a rider over eighteen years old who doesn't get paid to ride.

athletic: just what it says, but can also be a euphemism for "strong."

automatic changes (also easy changes): the horse can do a flying change of lead at the canter.

bombproof: very gentle and reliable—a bomb could go off and this horse would not spook.

brave, willing, honest: usually used to refer to horses used for jumping, meaning that they do not run out at the jumps. But also take these terms at face value.

brilliant: dazzling in terms of performance or appearance.

chrome: white markings. A horse with four white socks and a white star has "lots of chrome."

common: an everyday-looking horse. The common horse may be just what you want if you're looking to save money.

exp. rider: experienced rider. Take this seriously. The horse may be very strong, or difficult to control at times. If you are an experienced rider, these ads can often show you the way to a great buy, as the owner may be selling the horse because he's too strong for her or her child.

fancy: pretty.

flashy: lots of white.

goes on buckle: so gentle and calm you can "ride him on the buckle," or on a very long rein.

green: relatively untrained.

hot: excitable.

hunter: a horse suitable for riding to hounds (not a breed, although many hunters are Thoroughbreds.) If you want to jump, you're probably looking for a hunter or hunter-jumper.

in the ribbons: wins at horse shows.

lady's horse: gentle.

no vices: the horse does not crib, weave, bite, or kick.

professional: in these ads, this usually means a professional horse trainer or rider.

prospect: this means the horse, usually young, should be good at a particular sport, but has not had much training for it yet. You might see "excellent dressage prospect" to describe a horse who moves well.

puppy dog: sweet, kind.

sadly outgrown: another fairly straightforward term, meaning that the owner has either physically outgrown the horse or pony, or that she wants to ride at a higher level than the horse can do. If you don't need a horse who can jump 3'6", for example, and the horse's owner does, this can be a great way to find a mount.

scopey: the horse jumps well, with a lot of scope.

on top: this refers to the way horse genealogy is drawn. A horse who has "Zippo Pine Bar on top" has lineage back to the stallion Zippo Pine Bar in his sire's family. The dam's line goes on the bottom.

typey: true to type. A dishy face on an Arabian may lead to his being called "typey."

Keeping Your Horse for Less

Even before you've found your less-expensive horse, you need to find somewhere to keep him. There are a few ways to make horsekeeping less of a financial burden, but most of them require an outlay of time and effort on your part. One option is to board your horse at a cooperative barn. The barn itself may be owned by one of the boarders or leased from the owner. In an arrangement like this, there is usually no one manager. Instead, owners share duties on a weekly schedule. So if the barn has six horses and there are three owners, one person might have two days "on-duty" one week, and three the next. For this to work, everyone has to be somewhat flexible, which can be very difficult given horses' predilection for routine. Trying to keep horses in stalls in a cooperative setting can be difficult, but it can work.

In the summer, this could be a typical routine: The horses are out to pasture at night, when it is cooler. In the morning, the owner on duty comes in, and fills the horse's buckets with feed and water. She then brings in the horses, checking each one for injuries or lameness. When she returns in the afternoon, she feeds and waters again, then turns the horses out. Next, she cleans their stalls, sweeps the aisles, and performs other barn maintenance checks. She fills the water troughs, and leaves the horses out. The next person on duty returns the next morning to resume the routine.

With horses on 24-hour turnout, the on-duty day can be somewhat simpler. The person on duty arrives in the morning, and checks on all the horses, looking each one over for any wounds or odd behavior. She may have to bring one or two in for additional fly spray or to put ointment on a scrape. Then she fills the troughs, and leaves, to return in the afternoon and repeat the routine.

Wintertime makes either situation a bit more complex. Horses on field board need blanket checks and changes if they have gotten wet, as well as the constant dance of the hay bale. While hay bales are often wasteful, since horses trample them and spread a lot of the hay in the resulting mud, hay bales often provide the easiest way to get pasture horses the large amount of hay they need in the winter, and many who keep their horses out depend on them. But they require a tractor to transport them, and in a smaller operation, horses may simply need extra flakes of hay tossed to them each day, which becomes the responsibility of the on-duty caretaker.

For horses that are turned out during the day in winter, when it is warmer, the on-duty person arrives early in the morning, feeds, then turns the horses out after blanketing each one to his or her owner's specifications. Blanketing offers a range of choices, and many owners have strong feelings about the subject. Also, each horse is different. Your hefty draft cross may seem happy and warm with no cover at all while his Thoroughbred pasture mate shivers in 50° drizzle. Some owners clip their horses, who then need an underblanket as well as a turnout rug, while others let the natural coat grow, so their horses really take only a waterproof breathable, unless it gets to a certain temperature, in which case. . .

This is why charts are crucial in cooperative barns. Each owner should draw up her own preferences (dry-erase boards are great for this, since preferences tend to change). Each horse gets a large space on the board. If a horse is on supplements, these can be noted. And the whole blanket preference problem can be addressed here as well, for example: "If it's rainy and below 40, please put Sabine's waterproof over her rug. But if it is clear and cold (below 40), just the rug is fine. Harvey does not need anything unless it's wet—then, he needs the breathable."

As in any boarding situation, a dry-erase message board for riders to leave one another messages is crucial. This can be a place for each horse's veterinarian's contact information, as well as the number of the nearest large animal clinic. And every owner's information should be prominently posted. Don't forget owners' work and cell phone numbers, and e-mail addresses if the barn has an e-mail alert system. (Just don't leave too much information about your horse's breeding up—this can be overly helpful to a possible thief.)

Working for Board

Some boarding stables allow boarders to work off their horse's keep. Indeed, boarders or students working is how some places keep things going. A student might arrive for a lesson, and then spend an hour or two mucking stalls to pay for it. Or turnout would take place

Mucking stalls is one way to help pay for board.

on a rotating basis, with boarders or students taking different days of the week. In these situations, often one person is in charge to coordinate the complicated schedule. Also, they typically work the most efficiently when all the horses involved are school horses.

Other barns prefer not to have help other than their staffers, in order to make things somewhat more consistent for their boarders. If your barn manager likes to have the same hired crew doing things around her barn every day, don't be offended. It's just a preference for lack of change in daily routine. Especially at show or breeding barns, or other barns where horses may have complex supplement and feeding schedules, it helps to have the same staff who are accustomed to each horse's peculiarities and abreast of daily changes.

On the other hand, if you can work off at least some of that board, it can have real advantages for you. The economic one is obvious—this may allow you to give your horse stall board when you might only have afforded field board otherwise. Don't be surprised, however, if the only job available to you is mucking stalls. That's not usually anyone's favorite part of horse care, and it's the likeliest to get handed down. Even mucking stalls, though, has educational value. You learn how to keep a stall clean, which horses are picky about where they eliminate, and how to detect illness from manure. Being able to appreciate a well-cleaned stall will give you another way to evaluate other barns, and getting used to what healthy manure looks like can even alert you to changes in your horse's well-being.

But there are other ways to earn money towards your horse's keep. If you are at a teaching barn and reasonably far along in your own training, ask about giving "up-down" lessons, or the first round or so. Many trainers prefer to teach their students right from the start, but if you have been with the trainer for some time, she might let you teach, since your ways will be most like hers. These lessons are crucial, as they are when students learn about grooming, leading a horse, and so on.

Also, ask about barn maintenance. If a fence needs repair, or new saddle racks need to be made for the tack room, you could offer your labor free in return for board. You might help offer to run errands. Every barn manager spends a lot of time shuttling back and forth between the feed store and the barn, and if she is willing to relinquish this task, it's something you can easily take over (if you happen to have a truck or can drive the farm truck). Other opportunities are mowing, helping on days when the vet comes, especially if your barn has a lot of pasture horses who need to be wormed all at once, cleaning school tack, and general barn cleaning. Often, barn managers count sweeping aisles and other tasks as daily work, but slightly less frequently performed tasks like scrubbing buckets, cobwebbing, and cleaning the tack room or bathrooms may be welcome ways for you to help earn your horse's board.

You can also build or paint jumps, maintain trails, weed, or help with barn landscaping. Use your imagination and your knowledge of your own barn's situation to realize what it needs, and how you can help best. Managers are often amenable to swapping labor for board instead of paying for these services.

Lesson Board

You're not the only one who can help foot that board bill. Your horse can pitch in by becoming a part-time school horse. Obviously, your horse needs to be very

Allowing your horse to be used in lessons can sometimes help bring the board bill down.

reliable and sound, since he will be subjected to all kinds of riders as a lesson horse. That unsettling habit of bucking at the canter may be something you can handle, but could hurt an unsuspecting beginner. For one thing, you need a barn that gives lessons. And, most important, you need to be comfortable with the person who gives those lessons and the way in which your horse will be used. You don't want to find your semi-navicular trail horse being used to jump or your spooky horse heading out to the trail with a novice rider on his back. Some owners resist having their horses used for beginner lessons, since poor hands can harm a horse's mouth. Also, many owners do not like their horses to be jumped in lessons, since jumping carries with it an added risk of injury.

But if you respect the trainer who will be using your horse, and can be very clear about what activities he can be used for (as well as what tack should be used on him), lesson board can work well. Discuss a schedule with the trainer. You might know you will want to ride on Wednesdays and the weekend. Then your horse could be used for one lesson on Tuesdays and Thursdays, with Mondays and Fridays off.

You can ask that the trainer use your horse for lessons that work with what the two of you are working on as well. If your goal is not to rush jumps, ask her to put him through plenty of flatwork that will help his pacing. You may even prefer that your horse only be used for beginners (less exercise for him) or only advanced riders (less chance of his mouth being pulled on). Some riders only want their horses used for ground lessons, like bathing and polo-wrapping. (But don't be surprised if the economic payoff for those types of lessons is not as great.) The key is that you trust the trainer. Then you know that your horse is in good hands, and that he is not having anything asked of him that you would not ask of him yourself.

Field Board

Field board, or pasture board, is just what it sounds like. It means your horse is out to pasture all the time. He doesn't have his own stall, but is always turned out with one or more horses. Field board is always cheaper than stall board, for obvious reasons. Your horse will not have to be brought in and out daily, no stalls need to be mucked for him, and in many cases, he will not receive grain.

Field board has non-monetary advantages as well. In addition to being the most natural way to keep a horse, and the way many owners prefer, field-boarded horses seem to colic less often and weather the seasons with less human involvement, such as blanketing. A "hot" horse may benefit from field board and be much more even-tempered than he would be in a stall. Also, you know that he is not cooped up and is closer to his natural state.

The down sides are that your horse is not always right in the barn, and that he will be harder to groom after a rainstorm and subsequent roll in the mud. In the winter, you must take care not to over-groom a field-boarded horse, as he needs the essential oils he produces to stay warm. It is tough to compete year-round on a horse who lives outside since he should remain unblanketed whenever possible. This means clipping is a bad idea, although a strip or trace clip (in which the horse keeps most of his winter coat) can be all right on a horse who is, for example, foxhunted frequently or otherwise works hard through the winter.

There are as many types of field board as there are stall board. Some barns have fairly plush field board arrangements, sometimes called "premium field board." Then your horse might receive grain twice a day, get blanketed by the barn staff, and will probably have a run-in shed for inclement weather. There might even be a small shed or barn by your horse's field so that you don't have to bring him all the way in to tack up.

Usually, though, field boarders do not get grain, just grass and then plenty of hay in the winter. It is nice if the hay is under cover, but many places prefer to put round bales out in racks or on the ground, even though this is

Field board is typically less expensive than stall board.

fairly wasteful as the hay gets trampled. Some places have running streams, but there should always be a trough as a backup, and that trough should always be clean and full. Salt blocks and mineral blocks should be placed out for the field boarders as well as stall boarders. At the minimum, your horse should have a good stand of trees for protection from the weather, but a run-in shed is preferable, and it should be one that can accommodate all the horses in the field. This may be a two-stall arrangement for a paddock with only a couple of boarders, or a long shed for a real herd. There should also be some kind of "sick bay" arrangement, just in case your horse hurts himself or gets ill and needs to be on stall rest.

But don't expect too much if you are field boarding. Some places even have restrictions on which barn amenities field boarders can use, like the ring or the barn cross-ties. (Although this can indicate a sort of nasty hierarchy among people you may want to avoid in a boarding establishment, it does happen.) Plan to do your own blanketing and any special feeding your horse might need. It's not really expected for the barn manager or staff to wander out into the field to blanket your horse, although any understanding manager would make exceptions if you simply could not make it out and your horse was shivering. If you decide he needs corn oil or other supplements, you may have to give them yourself, probably separating your horse from his buddies to do it. If you are field boarding, you will need some extra time when your horse needs extra attention.

Another thing to consider when field boarding is

how you feel about large groups of horses. Chances are that yours will be more scuffed up than he would be in a stall (although even horses with limited turnout get into scuffles). Naturally, there will be some rivalry in a herd. In situations such as a new hay bale being placed outside, or just a tense moment at the water trough, horses will be horses, and yours may wind up with some nicks and scrapes. A field boarder also needs to be easy to catch, especially if the field is large. If your horse is tricky about this, think hard before turning him out on thirty acres with twelve buddies.

Less Expensive Stall Board

Stall board is very helpful if you show your horse or have another reason for his needing to remain as clean as possible or clipped. It is nice to know right where you'll find your horse when you come in, and for him to have his own place. Stall board saves time, since you do not have to trek out to the field to find your horse. Also, a horse who has an old injury or needs enforced rest might benefit from living in a stall. And any horse who has special feed needs is more easily fed inside.

Stall board is typically more expensive than field board at the same barn, though, since it means someone has to clean the stalls and feed the horses. Most stall boarding arrangements are combined with at least some turnout, which requires labor from people who turn the horses out and bring them back in.

Stall-kept horses benefit from turnout. A little freedom makes them less sour and less likely to develop stall vices like weaving.

It is possible to moderate the high cost of stabling a horse with a cooperative plan or in some way swap labor for board, as described earlier. Barns farther away from cities are sometimes cheaper than comparable, but closer-in facilities, and if you are willing to drive a bit more, you may be able to find a deal on stall board.

At Home

Keeping horses at home is not practical for many riders. Some people may be the only horseperson in the family, or simply not have the space, means or time to care for the horses on their own property. If you have the room, time, and inclination, horsekeeping at home is its own reward. For many people, the idea of waking up and seeing their horses peacefully cropping grass outside the window is very appealing Keeping your horses with you gives you the chance to get to know them even better, and the ability to memorize their habits and understand their personalities. Even on the coldest winter days, you will be able to see your horse and give him a carrot, and you will always know he is getting the best care you can give.

Sometimes keeping your horse at home can be less costly than boarding him. The time involved, however, is much greater, and your place will be devoted to horses, whether it feels that way at the outset or not. If you live in the country or have plenty of acreage, making your place into a horse farm requires, at the minimum, sufficient grazing space and some kind of shelter or place to store equipment and tack. If you plan to keep your horses out, you don't really need a barn, although it is nice to have one, even if it is more of a shed to tack up in. Also, should one of your horses get sick or hurt, it is useful to have a place for him to recuperate. It's also nice to have a place to cross-tie your horse to tack up and for the vet and farrier. And of course, without at least a good stand of trees, horses will need a run-in shed of their own.

Remember that tack and feed should be stored in a separate room, so that the horses cannot get at them. It's a good idea to keep hay, which is flammable, away from the barn if you can. (This can help keep your insurance premiums down as well.)

The variety of structures people erect to keep horses is vast, and there are many excellent books on barn building and maintenance that will give you further information. Architects who specialize in equestrian facilities are also good resources. (Just remember to add at least one more stall than you think you will need. Horses tend to accumulate around those willing to have them.) Methods of pasture care and rotation vary greatly according to climate and location. Local or state agricultural organizations are often the best resources for information on how to plan and grow your fields.

Assuming you have everything in place, there are a few ways to keep the cost of horsekeeping at home to a minimum. For one, don't feed hay on the ground. It's easy, but it's also a waste of hay and money when the horses drop and tramp on it. The investment you make in a hay rack will pay you back in salvaged hay. (Dirty, trodden hay can be very inviting to parasites.) In addition, you don't often have to grain your horses if they are not in heavy work. Just hay is fine for many horses; ask your veterinarian, but staying away from expensive supplements and feed can keep costs down.

Bedding does not have to be the extra-fancy, large

cedar shavings that smell and look so appealing. Shavings can be sold as compost if you do decide to go this route.

You can bed a horse on straw (it is harder to muck, but works fine). Straw offers good drainage and also looks fresh if it is kept clean. It also dries quite easily. Some horses will, however, eat straw, and straw does tend to make the manure pile bigger. Straw is easier on the pastures when spread, and can be recycled to mushroom farms.

But probably the biggest savings to having your horse at home is that you are the barn help. If you're cleaning stalls, blanketing, and waiting for the farrier yourself, you're not paying someone else for these tasks. The down side is that after cleaning stalls, sweeping aisles, and refilling water troughs, you may not feel much like riding, especially if you are also holding down a day job. But all of these things can bring you closer to your horse. When you spend so much time around the barn, you can't help but know him better than you would if he were boarded somewhere.

You can keep costs down by how you arrange your horsekeeping environment. Pretty white Man-O-War fencing surrounds many of our dream farms and works very well, but it's very expensive, as is post and rail fencing. Electric fencing, while not always the prettiest, is less costly. If properly installed, it's safe, effective, and can look perfectly clean and neat. You can also use a combination—consider board fencing facing the road, with electric fencing on the less-visible sides.

Electric fencing works because horses stay away

from it if they have ever been given the mild shock it transmits. Most horses will figure this out their first time in electric fencing, but it's a good idea to walk your horse around any paddock encased in wire his first time in it. You want him to realize where the boundaries are. Barbed wire is cheap but it is generally not recommended, given how easily horses get tangled in it and injured.

Because of the economics of horse ownership, cost has to be a primary consideration for any horse owner. But it does not need to direct our lives. With a little care toward keeping costs down, responsible horse owners can enjoy their horses and feel confident that they will be able to take care of any problems that arise. Remember the horseman's saw: the money you're saving in therapy bills by being around horses can easily support your passion for riding.

Without **Your Own** Horse

6

Being a horseless horseman can be tough. You have to find a horse to spend time with before you can concentrate on horsemanship. But if you're devoted to an equestrian sport or simply to spending time with horses, there are many ways to do so. The key is not to turn anything down. Even if your eventual goal is to buy a Quarter Horse and compete in barrel racing, you can still benefit from volunteering at a farm for retired Standardbreds. Everything you learn about horses from being around them can be used later. Experience makes a horseperson, and the old saying, "They all have four legs and a tail," is a good one to keep in mind when seeking exposure.

If you are interested in owning a horse eventually, it can help to spend some time in the horse world before you start shopping. Leasing a horse or working at a stable may make you realize that you're not quite ready for the financial or time investment that horse ownership demands. Spending time with horses may actually let the pressure off of finding one of your own. You can horse-shop without urgency while leasing a horse, or while you're getting your riding time in at a local trail ride barn.

Volunteering

You will find more horses to ride if you keep an open mind about volunteering in general. Who needs help in your local horse community? Ask local farriers and trainers, vets and even equine insurance agents. All these people visit barns daily, and may have heard about a horse who needs exercise or one up for lease.

Paying jobs like grooming offer time around horses as well, but if you already have a job and are only looking for recreational horse time, volunteer for jobs like grooming, barn chores, and helping with lessons. Your "pay" can be in time around horses. Treat these volunteer opportunities as you would a real job, however. If you offer to help your trainer with a group lesson, be thorough in your assistance throughout the lesson, from

tacking up to cooling out. That way, you will see more of the process, and you'll also demonstrate how serious you are about wanting to increase your horse time.

Volunteering for therapeutic riding programs or rescue barns is an excellent way to spend time with horses. If you volunteer at a barn as a helper for a handicapped riding program, riding is sometimes a fringe benefit. You might be able to act as a side walker or general helper. Each student can require up to four assistants—a riding instructor, a leader, and two side walkers—so these

Just because you can't own a horse doesn't mean you can't befriend one.

programs are often understaffed and seeking help. Participating in the program will not only allow you to help people who truly benefit from riding, it will also allow you to be around horses. If you are a handicapped rider yourself, consider spending time at the barn helping out after your lesson.

Ask the program coordinators if their horses need to be worked outside the lessons. Often, there are horses at handicapped riding programs who are there on trial while the staff sees if they will be suitable for disabled riders. It could be your job to try these horses in various situations, testing their spooking level. You may be asked to do basic "bombproofing," such as riding a horse along a road, or exposing him to everyday "spookers" like rustling trees, moving creeks, and other horses in a field. But you can also help a program like this by riding with braces or other devices that the riders may have that could potentially scare the horses. This way, the horses grow accustomed to the extra equipment and are less likely to act up when a rider mounts.

Horses are used for therapy for at-risk children, mental patients, and addicts as well. These people may learn about horses as a means to facilitate self-reliance, and to help them learn about taking care. Some patients even groom horses as a relaxing tactic. If you are near one of these programs, you could help teach the patients horse care, and assist in leading and assigning horses. Access to the programs' horses might serve as one of your benefits.

Equine rescue facilities also need volunteers. These

are places that house neglected and abused horses. Some of them adopt out the horses after they have healed physically and mentally, and some simply serve as havens. In general, rescue farms always need help, both financial and physical. If you can give time, there are always chores to be done, from envelope stuffing and other help with fundraising to basic barn chores.

Positions at rescue farms may not come with riding privileges, since the horses at the barn may have been abused beyond their ability to serve as mounts. A horse who has been starved for a year will have to heal for quite some time before someone can climb onto his back. But there are other rewards to being around abused animals. You can be the person who helps restore their trust in people, something they will have to regain before anyone can imagine riding or using them. By "adopting" one of the horses, even if you can't technically take him home, you can help him realize that people are not all as evil as the ones who hurt him. The management of the facility will help guide you, and you can reap the benefits of knowing a horse and knowing that you've helped.

Volunteering at a rescue farm is not for the timid, since the horses have often survived unimaginable cruelty, and bear both physical and behavioral scars. It can also be difficult to become attached to a horse only to see him adopted by someone else. But gratis work for a rescue organization can benefit you as well as the horses you assist, because you get to spend time with horses at their weakest, getting to know more about their behavior than most people do. And you are helping prepare a horse for a life outside of the rescue farm, where he can be a normal horse again.

Search and Rescue

Mounted search and rescue teams, or posses, are typically made up of people with their own horses who help local authorities look for lost hikers. They are trained to ride in bad weather to assist in finding the missing, and then to help in any way needed. They often transport injured people to safety, either by litter or on horseback.

Even though many squads are made up of horse owners, some use volunteers without horses to assist in missions. Also, if some members cannot go on a mission, you could ride one of their horses as a similarly trained rider. Search and rescue horses, like police horses, need to be trained to be ridden in any circumstance, such as rough terrain and heavy rain. Learning to be a litter-bearer is also a skill for a horse. You may be able to help with this training if you are willing to put in time and effort to school others' horses in facing adversity under saddle.

Leasing

Leasing is one of the most popular ways to enjoy a horse that does not belong to you. In a lease situation, you pay to ride a horse owned by another rider. Regular leases are fairly straightforward in that you basically act as the horse's owner, and may pay his board, farrier, and vet bills in return for being allowed to ride him when you like. Sometimes there is a leasing fee on top of this, especially for horses you plan to show. Leasing is an excellent option for a rider who knows she wants to ride, but is not entirely ready for the responsibility of horse ownership. A year of leasing will usually tell you whether you want to look for your own horse, or back off and keep riding others'.

Many people show leased horses. They may be leasing a campaigner in a new division for them, and will be ready to bring their own horse along later. If you are a competitor, this gives you time to check out a new sport or discipline without buying an expensive horse with a track record of success in that sport.

A half-lease offers similar benefits to full leasing, but with less cost. You and the owner (or the other half-leaser) each ride part of the week. Then the horse gets at least one day off. Some riding academies or stables half-lease school horses. These programs are often effective because with precedent, there is a tried system in place for how the half-lease works. And since the horse is owned by a business, you will simply have to sign and abide by their customary agreement. Programs like these are a great way to start out, since you'll also be riding in an environment customized for arrangements like these.

Leases can be very effective and satisfying for all involved, but they also can be fraught with difficulty. Arguments over whose day it is, who is responsible for calling the vet about that possible lameness, and equipment use are, unfortunately, very common. But leasing is often the best possible avenue for the rider who is not yet ready to be a horse owner. The key is making sure that all parties have clear and reasonable expectations that can be met.

All arrangements should be discussed and written down. With your leasing partner, set to paper all the rules you want to make and abide by. These include simple scheduling things like riding times and equipment use. Do you each have your own saddle? Will you be sharing a bridle? How often does it need to be cleaned? If you only trail ride the horse, but your co-lessee jumps him, would you prefer if his forelegs were

If you co-lease a horse, be sure to discuss details, like whether the horse should be jumped.

wrapped? Should he be turned out in bell boots? Who will met the farrier? How can you remain in touch so that you don't take him for a four-hour trail ride the day before a big jumping lesson? You should each know the best way to reach each other to avoid conflicts and disappointments.

Walk away from the meeting with a clear schedule, and all the contact information. It's important that you be able to reach each other not only in scheduling matters, like swapping days, but to report on the horse. If he seemed sore to you, or seems to need more blanketing that you'd originally thought, you need to be able to communicate that to your leasing partner. Remember that you will probably not see her very much since you will necessarily be riding at different times.

The legal aspect of leasing also needs to be set in writing to protect everyone involved. You may want to consult a lawyer who specializes in equestrian affairs, or a book about the legal aspects of the horse world for some sample forms. The basic form should involve answers to who pays for major veterinary care and upkeep. Sometimes you can figure out who caused the reason for care, such as a cut sustained on a trail ride. But often, horses come in from the pasture with an injury requiring medical attention, or simply get sick. Then the lessee is not necessarily to blame. If you're in a half-lease situation, consider sharing paying for an insurance policy, whether for sickness or mortality.

Horse ownership carries with it much legal responsibility. In some areas, you can be held accountable if

With common goals and understanding, two people can share the same horse.

your horse bites someone across a fence. In the case of something like this, who is financially responsible? Just as you sign release waivers at a boarding or rental stable, seek legal advice for what you are and are not responsible for, whether you are the lessee or the owner.

Whether or not the horse's owner is one of his riders, she should be consulted as to the restrictions on the horse. How does she feel about his jumping? How high? Are there certain bits she does not want used on him? Where can he be boarded? How does she feel about him being trailered to shows or elsewhere? Whose job is it to make sure his worming schedule and other basic veterinary needs are met? Some owners do not want their horses ridden bareback, and others prefer that they only be shown a certain number of weekends in a season. It's also important to discuss which professionals will be used. If the horse has a regular farrier and veterinarian, the owner might prefer that those people keep seeing him, even if you've used different ones in the past.

Riding Vacations

The idea of riding vacations calls to mind the dude ranch, which for a long time was the most popular way for city people, or dudes, to spend some time on horseback. Dude (or vacation) ranches are still popular, and provide an excellent way for both novice and experienced riders to spend long hours in the saddle. But nowadays there are all kinds of riding vacations. They may not be the cheapest way to get to ride, but being on an equestrian holiday allows you to enjoy both your hobby and your time off. For people who do not have their own horses, riding vacations are a good way to get that rare spell of daily riding in.

Many equestrian vacations include options for non-riding spouses or family members, and some are geared to different skill levels as well. There is a wide range of vacations centered around horses, from visiting someone's ranch and riding with them there to touring a country on horseback. It can also be a good way to try a different sport or discipline, and take a break from the dressage arena to ride Western for a week.

Check with the company you're booking with to see what kind of skill level you need. In general, a riding vacation is not necessarily the best way to learn to ride, although many offer do instructional clinics before a vacation starts. If you're traveling with non-riding family members, consider visiting a ranch or other one-site vacation, because the prospect of long days in the saddle is not always a good introduction to riding, and you may end up turning family members away from the very sport you hoped they would learn to love. At a dude ranch or other vacation farm, you'll usually get to ride all you like, while the people in the family who don't ride (yet!) will spend some time on horseback, but also doing other things.

Riding Academies

Where you take lessons can affect how much you ride. As discussed in Chapter 1, there are some ways to evaluate instructors and lesson facilities for safety and what the lessons are like. If you don't have your own horse, though, these factors become increasingly important, along with one other: how much can you ride?

This varies a great deal among riding stables. Some places provide you with a tacked-up horse, you ride in your lesson, and then need to return the horse to a groom to be untacked, etc. This has merit if you're trying to squeeze a lesson into an already crowded schedule, but is disappointing if you are using your lessons as a way to be around horses. At some barns, the groom program is designed to satisfy that, and so you're handing your horse off to someone who is working for her lessons, or simply helping out to be around horses.

If you're seeking extra time with your lesson mount, say so. Many barns have programs by which if you are a student, you can do practice rides during the week. You'll usually pay a fee for each time you ride, and may not be able to specify which horse you'd like. Typically, there is no jumping allowed during these rides, but they are an excellent way for you to get more saddle time, and just more horse time in general. You may have to reach a certain level of riding in order to be able to ride unsupervised, and know enough about horse care that you put the horse and equipment away properly and cleanly.

Both large riding academies and smaller private stables have ways in which you can ride more than just in your lesson. At a private barn, you may simply be able to work out an arrangement with your instructor. Perhaps she has enough horses for her daily lesson schedule, and will allow you to ride one.

If your stable does not have a practice ride program, get organized. Ask other students if they would be interested in paying for practice rides and having greater access to the lesson horses. If the management realizes that a whole group of students wants to spend more time with their horses, they may see it as an opportunity to expand their program and offerings (as well as to collect lesson fees).

It's easy to get attached to lesson horses. Of course, good riders can ride anything, but there is also a special bond between horses and people that sometimes crops up even in a once-a-week lesson situation. If you have a good ride on a certain horse, and feel like you have "clicked" with him, by all means request him the next time. But bear in mind that your riding will improve, and you will be a more versatile rider, if you spend time with different horses. One of the merits to being a horseless rider is that it often forces you to spend time with different horses. As you do so, you may come to realize more fully what you want from a horse.

Unfortunately, once it does become time for you to buy a horse, that schoolmaster you fell in love with will probably not be for sale. Good lesson horses are thin on the ground, and many trainers will not want to give theirs up.

Getting the Most from Lessons

All riders in training depend upon their lessons to help them progress. But horseless riders do in particular, since for many lessons provide their only riding time. Lessons become even more important when they not only help you become a better rider, but let you know how involved you want to become in the world of horses.

There are usually three kinds of lessons: private, group, and semi-private. Each has its advantages. Private lessons are usually the most expensive because they require the instructor's undivided attention be on you. It is nice to take private lessons when you are looking for that kind of focus, or when you're getting ready for a specific riding event. In semi-private lessons, you share your trainer with one other rider, who should be near the same skill level you are. (Steer clear of trainers who say they can teach two very differently skilled riders—they're basically teaching two lessons at once, which is not productive for anyone.) You'll ride the same exercises, and each of you will have some time during which the trainer comments on what you're doing. These are often only a little bit cheaper than private lessons, but it's often nice to watch someone else ride a pattern or jump you're aiming for yourself. In a group lesson, more riders work on similar skills together. The actual number varies widely, as some places limit groups to five or six, and others get higher, often with an assistant trainer to help during them. These are typically the most economical way to go, but you do sacrifice some individual attention, and often the person having the most trouble receives the most instruction. On the other hand, you benefit from watching many people ride, and from a highly organized lesson in general.

Arrive early for your lessons. You won't be rushed as you tack up or even lead the horse you'll ride from the field or his stall. Consider stretching (see Chapter 7 for more on fitness for riding) before your lessons, so that you minimize the risk of injury and the risk that you will get really tired and want to stop riding before your lesson, typically an hour long, is over.

With a little bit of extra time, you can be ready to go when it's your turn, and maybe even watch some of the lesson before yours. (Some students prefer not to be observed, so check with your trainer first.) If you can, watching someone else ride can teach you about the horse they are on. Does he seem sulky? How is he responding to the rider on his back? What kind of tack is he in? It's not a good sign if he has all kinds of restraining or training devices on him. Observe how your trainer teaches other students. You may get some ideas for exercises you'd like to do, or horses you'd like to ride.

Don't worry about making mistakes during your lessons, as that's what the whole point is. Remember that you're there to learn. If you really do not feel that you're making progress, discuss this with your instructor. She may be seeing different advances than you are. It can be frustrating to take instruction with riding, especially if you're on different horses all the time. Sometimes you need someone to point out how well you're doing. Learning to ride various horses is in fact a skill of its own.

Keep a lesson journal. When you get home from your lesson, write down what you worked on that day. You can just use a notebook, or purchase one of the blank books expressly made for that purpose. Write down which horse you rode, and what you worked on. Did you

achieve the objectives set out for that day? It's a good idea not only to make notes about what you actually did—worked on trot to lope transitions, or on two-point position, but how it went for you and how well you worked with the horse you were on. So you might note that once you started looking up, the two-point became much easier, or that since the horse you rode was in a martingale today, he seemed to be more easily steered.

Make the most of time you have to talk with your trainer. Ask her which horse she thinks you do best on,

School horses are often the most available mounts for the horseless rider.

and why. Ask her what she thinks you should be working on, and if there are any ground (or mental) exercises that might improve your riding. If your barn does provide opportunities for practice rides, which horse does she think you should ride, and why? She can help you set up a sample hour so that you can maximize your riding time instead of wandering aimlessly around the ring (although some days aimless wandering may be exactly what you need). You develop "muscle memory" through repetition, so if she can give you some drills to work on you will be ahead of the game by your next lesson.

Catch-Riding and Borrowing Horses

Depending on what kind of work your trainer does, the route to a free ride is often through her. She can be instrumental in helping you find horses to catch-ride, which is a term for riding others' horses in shows and elsewhere. If you are a fairly experienced rider, your trainer may have some horses in training that need to be exercised. Even a novice rider can score some riding time on a horse who only needs walk-trot work, with your trainer supervising. If people leave their horses with her to be trained, they may have some days in their program when they need to be conditioned or longed, activities that you could handle. If you're farther along in your own training, you may be helping her school these horses.

In catch-riding for shows, which is where the term is most commonly used, you compete on horses belonging to other riders or to your trainer. These may include ponies that a child has outgrown but does not want to sell, or horses suited more to a certain division than their owner. You may catch-ride horses your trainer is bringing along as well, perhaps showing a horse in a local show to see how he does before your trainer takes him on a larger circuit.

Also look to your trainer for tips about other students who may need help with their horses. Pregnant or injured riders may need someone to work with their horses while they are out of the saddle, and students who are heading back to college may not be able to take their horses with them. You never know when someone will need her horse exercised, and your trainer often knows the most about what's happening in a barn. Especially if their non-riding is temporary, people may be more inclined to let you ride their horses than to lease them to someone. This is also more true if you would not charge anything. If you're available and free, you're at an advantage over others who may charge.

Even if it's only on a one-time basis, riding someone else's horse has some of the same guidelines as leasing him. You may not sign any waivers to ride the horse of an ill barnmate, but still be sure to ask her if she has any preferences about how he's ridden, what kind of tack to use, and if you may take him out on the trail. After your ride, be very scrupulous about grooming the horse—no girth marks or bridle marks. Pick out his hooves before you put him back in his stall or paddock. Make sure he has plenty of water. Replace all her equipment neatly, and clean any tack you've used. Make sure stirrups are back at the length you found them, and the saddle back under its cover. And always remember to say something nice about the horse, even if you found him difficult, and to thank his owner.

Trail Ride Barns

Trail ride barns are the modern equivalent of the livery stable. While there are still rental stables in some areas, rising insurance rates and an increasingly litigious society

have kept many horse people from venturing into the business of leasing horses by the hour. Instead, they own trail ride barns, where riders are typically guided along a trail by a barn employee, usually keeping to a walk. These barns may also offer services like pony rides for children and hay rides.

Taking these trail rides may not seem to be the best way to improve your equitation, but it all helps, and can be a nice way to see some of the countryside as well as getting some saddle time. If you are allowed to do so,

Renting horses at a trail ride barn can help you decide whether you're ready for a mount of your own.

select your own horse for the trail ride. Look for one who is not too listless or old, and one that does not have a lot of corrective tack on. Many of these horses spend their days on the exact same trails, so don't be too surprised if they seem less than fresh as you set out. They will appreciate a sensitive rider, though, and may react well to your seat and hands.

Also, talk to your guide. Which horse does she prefer? Why? Once you've demonstrated that you can ride on the trail, could you take one of the horses on a shorter, unguided trail ride? Find out more about the area as well as if there are any opportunities for freer riding at that barn. If you become familiar to the staff, they may keep you in mind when chances for less structured riding come along.

College Riding Teams

If you live near a college, university, or even a prep school with a riding team, you may be able to capitalize on their facilities. Many of these teams are filled with students who do not have their own horses. Their horse shows are judged solely on riding, in that each rider gets to the show and meets the horse she'll compete on for the first time that day. She mounts, rides, and moves on to the next horse. This does mean that schools involved in these programs have to have barns filled with available lesson horses.

These teams and programs are sometimes closed to

those outside the school community, but it is worthwhile to check into them. Some schools offer lessons at their barns, and this may entitle you to use the horses sometimes. You might also volunteer to help with their intercollegiate shows, which gives you more time around the barn and them some much-needed help on busy days.

Judging

Horse show judging at the highest levels is obviously for people who have been involved in the sport for years, typically starting as competitors. But local shows and events need judges as well, which is where you may come in. If there is a local point-to-point, for example, fence judges may be needed, since no one can see the whole field. In this case, you would stay by a certain fence and watch as horses came over it.

Youth organizations like 4-H also need judges for their shows. Evaluating children's abilities with their ponies is an important step for young horsemen, and you can help out by judging or advising these groups. As well as judging horsemanship and riding, you might participate in the quiz section of a youth organization's testing. Some programs have special training for their judges, which provides you with a learning opportunity at the same time you're preparing to help others. And it all gives you more time around horses and yet another entré into the world of horses that is right around you.

Even if you can't be a judge, volunteer your services

to show organizers. You could help with barn assignments, or with "traffic direction" as the classes are being called or trailers are being parked. Shows are hectic places, and those in charge often appreciate a helping hand. And you never know who you might meet with a spare horse for you to ride.

Horsey Pastimes

Just because you don't have your own horse does not mean you should not attend events geared toward those who do. If you love horses, it's fun to be at things centered around them, and again, you just never know whom you might meet who is looking for barn help or a catch-rider. So keep an eye out.

A club can help facilitate this. If you know other riders who are in the same position you are, possibly from your lessons, consider forming a club. Being in a group will give you more visibility when you do something like approach the local trail riding barn to ask for group rates, or ask a mounted police officer to come to your barn to give a demonstration. It's also enjoyable to spend time with like-minded people. Even working out can be more fun (and you'll more likely do it) when you have a buddy who has a similar goal of becoming a fitter rider.

When an equestrian trade fair comes to your area, take your club and go. These are usually held in livestock arenas or conference centers, and feature all the latest products available to horse people. Often, hearing experts speak is included in the price of admission, so you may spend a day watching your favorite clinician, as well as seeing different breeds of horses and shopping. These fairs often have areas where local businesses put on displays as well, so they can be a good place to discover riding opportunities you didn't know about.

Reading about the horse world is also a great way to get involved and find out everything horsey happening near you. Many equestrian areas have their own publications, but even if yours doesn't, national magazines are helpful. They keep you abreast of what is happening in the horse world at large, and provide you with questions to ask your instructor. You may see an exercise you like in an article, and use that during your next practice ride. Enjoy scanning the classifieds as well—it all makes you more well-versed in your sport. Obviously, book learning is no replacement for time in the saddle, but it does help, and you may uncover an idea or image that really helps your training.

Being without a mount can be frustrating, but it's also an opportunity to gain experience and education about many different facets of the horse world. And once you do own your own horse, you'll draw often on all the things you learned as a horseless rider.

Fitness for You and Your Horse

You work hard physically when you ride, and so does your horse. To decrease your risk of injury, and thus be able to enjoy your riding time more, you both need to be in shape. Keeping fit is a crucial part of equestrian sports. While riding itself may keep you in basic riding shape, there's more to staying in peak condition than just mounting and galloping off. We have much in common with our horses when it comes to conditioning, but there are salient differences.

Conditioning keeps your horse ready to work with you. It's often a stepping stone to achievement in a certain sport, but a fitness program for your horse has its

A horse who is in condition is much more likely to succeed at his sport.

own rewards as well. A fit horse is more likely to be strong and to stay sound. He will fare better in the winter months, and use his food more efficiently, just as a fit person does.

Horses are amazingly adaptable and forgiving creatures. Some will be pulled out of the field once a month for a ten-mile ride and be all right the next day. But although this kind of treatment is common, it's also unfair to the horse. You never know what day he's just not going to make it under duress, and without conditioning, his bones and muscles could suffer from work. Conditioning is your responsibility.

How It Works

In conditioning a horse, workouts demand more power and energy from the body in order to perform increasingly strenuous tasks. Conditioning improves your horse's fitness by adding the amount of stress you ask the horse's body to take. You need to provide this constructive stress without harming the horse. Once he recovers, you heighten his workouts and begin the cycle again. Over time, his body will respond to the challenge with increased muscle and wind. With proper rest, food, and preparation, your horse will become able to work for longer times and in more stressful situations.

Horses condition both anaerobically and aerobically. Instead of lifting weights as a person would for anaerobic conditioning, horses can be asked to perform the skill they'll be asked to do, like reining patterns or jumps. Conditioning means that muscles increase. You'll see the difference in your horse's shape as you work him. (Some people are more fanatic about their horse's body building than their own.) And their aerobic condition is improved through lots of trotting, with some walking and cantering. This is what endurance riders call LSD, or long, slow, distance work. This helps the heart, the horse's most important muscle, become stronger and able to help him carry you at different paces. It also becomes better at using energy.

Evaluating Your Horse's Condition and Weight

The first thing to do before starting a fitness program for your horse is make an appointment with your veterinarian. She can evaluate his preparedness to undertake the kind of training you have in mind, and help you set some goals for his progress. Specify the tasks that go with your sport, like jumping. Then ask your veterinarian what exercises can strengthen the muscles involved, so that your horse can avoid the back injuries many jumpers sustain. Be especially careful when conditioning a young horse, because without the benefit of history, it's more difficult to read his responses. Immature systems are at particular risk of injury, as well, so a veterinarian-authored program is especially important for a young horse.

While working on conditioning, you need to monitor your horse's weight. Even though the main goal of conditioning is to improve strength and stamina, not to regulate weight, a horse will have a much easier time getting and staying fit if he is in good flesh, or at an appropriate weight. An "average," or middle-of-the-road horse, will have a level back. There may be a flash of rib occasionally, but mostly ribs are invisible. In "winter weight," the horse may have a slight crease along the back. An old way of saying this is that you can "roll an egg down his back."

In a horse that is too thin, the back bone is prominent. His bones are visible, such as hip bones or pelvic bones. In some thin horses, the vertabrae can even be seen. An overly thin horse is already stressed by lacking the resources to brave weather and be ridden.

Overweight can be detrimental to horse health as well. In a fatter horse, the crease down the horse's back will become deeper, and the area around his tailhead will be padded with fat as well. It's unhealthy for horses to be overweight because it puts additional stress on the joints and heart, and makes it more difficult to move around. Founder, or laminitis, is also a real danger for the overweight horse. A pasture boarded horse heading into the winter can take more weight than you might like to see on him in the summer, but if your horse is getting truly fat, you should try to have him lose weight by putting him in a dry lot for some of the day, or cutting down his rations.

Calculating Your Horse's Fitness

If you become interested in conditioning, which will especially happen if you decide to try endurance riding or eventing, you will need expert guidance. But some of the principles used by endurance riders can help any rider give some specifics to her horse's condition. To use a stethoscope, ask your veterinarian or someone accustomed to using one to show you the first time. If you place a stethoscope on the left side of your horse's chest, near his girth, you should hear how many beats his heart makes in a minute.

If you undertake serious conditioning work, you may want to invest in a heart-rate monitor for your horse, which uses electrodes to determine exact heart rates. (These show the heart rate while the horse is exercising, and when you feel his pulse you are feeling it after the drop in heart rate caused by pulling up and stopping work.) But for most people, finding your horse's pulse and calculating his beats per minute will be sufficient. As discussed in Chapter 4, you can also take your horse's pulse by feeling it right in the edge of his jawbone. Count how many beats you feel in ten seconds, then multiply by 6 for the beats per minute. Most horses have a pulse rate between 30-45 (typically around 35) beats per minute when they are resting. Their heart rate can go up to around 230-250 beats per minute under maximum stress.

To improve cardiac condition, horses should have a working heart rate of around 120 beats per minute. And within fifteen minutes after the workout, an in-shape horse's pulse is around 60 beats per minute. If it takes longer than that, you may be working him too hard.

Warming Up and Cooling Down

Let's say your daily ride is about an hour. You will spend at least twenty to thirty minutes of that time warming your horse up and cooling him down. These transitional phases make it easier for your horse to climb to the level of performance you will be asking of him that day, and to descend back to a resting state. Without transitioning, you can hurt your horse's muscles and bones by jarring them into work.

Warming up can be done at the walk and then an easy trot. Don't just let your horse amble around aimlessly while you're warming him up. If you're riding in the ring, you could take a walk around a pasture or down the driveway for a warmup. In any case, your horse should step out nicely. Also, make plenty of turns and patterns, so that his mind does not turn off right when you need him to be sharpening up. While trotting, focus on the posting trot to start out—an English rider should not try to sit the trot until your horse's back is fairly well warmed up.

Cooling down is similarly crucial, as it allows your horse to make a safe shift back to rest. Horses who are not cooled down properly have increased risks of colic and azoturia, or "tying up," discussed later in this chapter.

Get to know what your horse looks like when he's breathing hard, and when he is at rest and has caught his breath. If he's still panting when you get back to the barn, he needs to be walked until he is breathing

normally. You can do this while you're on his back, but he may also appreciate a break from carrying you, so you can walk him in hand as well. Loosen his girth as you walk. Next you can take the saddle off, but leave the pad on, especially if it's cold out. You don't want to shock his sweaty back in the cold air.

If your horse is hot, hose him down with cool water. (The water that comes out of a hose should be fine unless it's extremely cold, as some well water can be.) Hose his legs, head, and chest before you do the body. Just keep running water over him and using a sweat scraper to remove it until his skin doesn't feel as hot. You can also tell how he's doing by feeling the water itself. If it's hot, so is your horse.

In cold weather, you can use a cooler (a lightweight blanket, often made of felt or wool) to keep him from getting a chill if he's gotten sweaty and hot. You'll know when he's really cooled out because his breathing will be normal, the veins in his neck will be down (they often get engorged during exercise), and his skin will feel normal temperature to the touch.

Horses need water after they work, but too much cold water can be uncomfortable for a hot horse to gulp. After a long gallop, or even a strenuous trail ride on a hot day, pay close attention to cooling him down. Try to give him cool or lukewarm water, and just let him have a little at first until he cools down. You can hand walk him and let him stop for a drink—about a gallon at a time—every few minutes. If your vet recommends it, you can put some electrolytes in the water.

Opposite page: Being hosed off feels good to a horse who has worked hard.

Conditioning Ideas

Conditioning programs vary widely depending on what you sport are preparing for. A reasonable goal for most horses is to trot a mile in ten minutes (6 mph) If your horse can accomplish that, he is in decent condition. If you want to participate in a sport like eventing or endurance riding, you will need a more specific and rigorous conditioning program. But if you want to depend on your horse for a day of ring work or a long trail ride, a benchmark of 6 mph will help you on your way.

Walking and trotting are the basic gaits of conditioning. When you start out, you will be walking a lot. Keep your horse moving—don't let him lag—at a good pace. At first, riding for fifteen or twenty minutes is enough. Each day, add on five or so more minutes. After seven to ten days of this, add some trot work. Mix it up: walk for five or so minutes, then trot, walk for ten, trot for ten. As you trot, practice collection and extension to add interest and variety. Don't be in too much of a hurry to trot the whole time, because steady increases will result in a fitter horse.

Keep in mind the importance of trail and field riding for conditioning purposes. Even if you and your horse spend most of your time in the ring, the field can offer excellent muscle building opportunities. Find some good hills, and ride them steadily. Going up and down provides strength training. Try different gaits—keep at a steady trot going up the hill, then a good working walk coming down.

Consider longeing as part of your back-to-work workout. While too much longeing will bore your horse and make you dizzy, it is a helpful conditioning tool, since it takes both aerobic and anaerobic strength to move in a small circle on the longe line. Twenty minutes is typically a good amount of time to work the horse and prevent him from getting sour. If you and your horse are used to using them, side reins can help build the rear muscles your horse needs to collect and carry himself. Some longeing in a field can help your horse be more surefooted when you ride him on similar ground.

Hill work is one of the most helpful conditioning tools.

Rest is important, both during a workout (as in letting your horse walk for a while before trotting more hills) and during his week. All horses should have at least one day off a week. Rest provides the time that horses need to recover from the constructive stress of one phase of conditioning and move onto the next.

Interval training—repeated bouts of high intensity exercise with intermittent rest periods—is popular in the human world these days, and some horses benefit from it as well. But it's mostly for racehorses and eventers. Even if you do it in your aerobics class, don't undertake interval training for your horse unless you've got a trainer who will monitor you closely, and measure all your horse's vitals during your workouts.

Consider field board on a large pasture with other horses as another way to help keep your horse in shape. Horse turned out like this move around more than their stabled counterparts. They walk up and down hills as a matter of course, and play pasture games that keep them moving all day. Ideally, this should be about three acres per horse for maximum roaming (and keeping fit) room. If you ride two or three days a week and your horse is on 24-hour turnout, you'll always be ahead of the game when you prepare for your sport.

Conditioning Problems

Extremes in weather conditions can affect conditioning your horse. If it's very hot out, watch your horse for signs of stress like panting, or cessation of sweating. As in people, these can mean heat exhaustion. Don't go for too long a ride in the heat, as you may need to get back to the barn if your horse seems exhausted. And always be sure your horse has plenty of water available so he stays hydrated.

As you ride in the winter, keep your horse going so that he doesn't get too chilly, but be very careful—overworking him can make him so sweaty that he'll be cold and wet, and thus very hard to cool down. If you've clipped your horse, use a quarter sheet to keep his rear end and hindquarters warm while you work. (Some of these have room for the rider as well, so you can keep cozy too.)

After working your horse, watch out for azoturia, also called tying up or Monday morning sickness. This occurs when an in-shape horse gets kept in a stall for a day without a corresponding reduction in grain rations. His hindquarters may spasm and then become immobilized. Watch out for dark urine, stiffness behind, and general distress. Call the vet right away if you notice any of these things.

Undertaking any conditioning program means you should be vigilant about monitoring your horse for signs of overdoing it. These include weight loss, ring sourness, dull coat, and heat in his legs. Vary your routine to keep him happier both mentally and physically, and call your veterinarian if he really begins seeming different from his usual self, like if he stops eating or showing any interest in his surroundings and companions.

Dehydration is one of the great dangers of strenuous work. Horses need enough water in their systems for their bodies to function properly. Horses can get dehydrated from sweating profusely, which you'll notice, or from a consistent cycle of sweating and drying, which is harder to detect. Signs of dehydration include hard manure balls, loss of skin elasticity, and colic. You can "pinch test" your horse to see if he's dehydrated. Take a pinch of skin on his shoulder. It should snap right back— you won't be able to see where you've pinched. If it stays pinched, he may be dehydrated. Just remember that

A thick fleece pad helps absorb moisture from perspiration, which can increase during conditioning work.

normally a horse will drink around five gallons of water a day, but he may need up to fifteen or twenty gallons if he's working hard in hot weather. He should always have fresh, clean water available.

A horse with back pain, which can be a result of overexertion or not having warmed up enough, will generally "tell" you with his behavior. Besides lameness or obvious distress when saddled or mounted, a horse with back pain may stand oddly. Or he may not want you to pick up his feet, since that would make him use his back in a way that might be uncomfortable for him. He'll also move stiffly—anything to avoid stressing the already sore areas. Even his playful bucking may seem constrained.

Things that can alleviate or help heal a sore back are plenty of turnout, or even pasture board for a while. Check that his saddle fits. Don't jump him, and keep his workouts really light (no hills, no extended trots or canters) until he feels better. Strive for a rounded frame, whether you're longeing or riding him. Walk him plenty. Even if your horse doesn't have a chronic problem, he might like some heat on his back after a long or tiring workout. You can soak a wet towel and apply that to his back under a liner (like a plastic garbage bag) with a cooler on top keeping everything in place.

Opposite page: To keep
limber and supple, do
some stretching exercises
before riding.

Conditioning for You

You owe it to your horse to stay in good physical condition. It's easier for him to carry a fit rider, because your ability to avoid bouncing on his back is tied to your holding yourself up with good stomach and back muscles. Riding itself will keep your riding skills sharp, but to maximize your time in the saddle, working out on the ground helps.

Being fit also makes you a better rider. You can ride for longer periods of time when you're in shape. A fit jumper rider, for instance, won't fall forward or back so much because she can support herself over the jumps and on the other side. Cantering for longer is easier on someone who is in good cardiac shape. A stronger rider's back hurts less, and she won't grip the horse's sides as much as someone who is not in good physical condition. Even the fittest riders get sore after an exceptionally long day in the saddle, but if you are in shape, you can expect more from your horse and yourself.

If you have ever felt winded after cantering around the ring more than twice, you may need more aerobic work. If you always feel sore after you ride, you might need to concentrate on strengthening certain muscles. If you set fitness goals, your doctor can help you work out a strengthening routine for specific muscle groups or cardiac ability. Knee, ankle, and back pain are all common in equestrians. Flip through any horse equipment catalog and you will see products designed to help stabilize joints and the back. It's more effective to keep

these areas strong in the first place than to try to fix them later.

Rider Conformation

Just as your horse's conformation affects his way of going, as discussed in Chapter 5, yours can affect your riding. Experience and time in the saddle work to overcome any physical shortcomings, but if you don't have the long-legged, trim build so suited to riding, you may have a slightly more uphill process to riding fitness than someone born with those qualities. Since some competitive riding focuses on appearance, many people worry a lot about how they look on their horses. It's understandable to want to present an appealing picture, but the most important reason to stay in shape for riding is to improve your riding itself. Different body types, however, sometimes require different regimens.

If your body tends toward the pear-shaped, you're suited to horseback riding, but you will not want to get out of balance because of differently proportioned top and bottom areas. With shorter legs, you may benefit from a shorter-barreled horse, so that the horse can "hear" your legs, even though they don't wrap all that far around. If your legs are long, but your torso is shorter, you may feel like you need to lean forward all the time. You may do better on a horse who isn't already heavy on the forehand. If you're petite, you don't necessarily need a small horse; the size of your ideal mount depends on your strength. On the other hand, you'll also look fine on a pony or a dainty Arabian. Like the shorter-legged rider, you'll just need to focus on "sitting deep" as you ride for maximum connection to your horse.

Weight

As it is with weight in every sport, the jury is still out on whether being overweight is detrimental to equestrians. Being overweight can make it harder to keep your balance in the saddle, and larger thighs make it more of a challenge to keep your legs in the most secure positions. Many people who might not fit the slim societal ideal, however, are excellent riders.

Some heavier riders prefer heavier horses, such as draft horses or draft crosses. But other breeds can carry larger riders as well if their conformation permits. Often a shorter back and strong legs on a horse will be conducive to carrying more weight.

Weight is secondary to fitness for riders. It's generally better to be in shape and a little heavy than it is to be out of shape and risk hurting your horse's back. Some rental stables and riding vacation stables have weight limits for riders, usually around 200 pounds. Any rider who hits her horse in the back is hurting him, but someone who weighs more can inflict even more damage. Staying at a healthy weight is good for you and your horse, but don't let a few extra pounds stop you from enjoying your favorite pastime.

Nutrition Supplements and Nutrition

A diet for riding is much like that for any other sport. Minimize sugars and too much fat in favor of densely packed nutritious meals. It's often hard to have a balanced diet and ride because of time constraints—by the time you've gone to work, ridden, and gotten home from the barn, a gourmet menu may be the last thing on your mind. It's much easier to order out. Eating well pays off in fitness, though, and makes it easier to keep your weight at a healthy level.

When you're going to spend the day at the barn, take a sandwich and some fruit instead of ordering out. Pizza places love barns, since they're always full of hungry riders. And horse shows are famous for their state-fair booths with fried egg sandwiches and hot dogs for sale. Defend yourself against these fatty menaces by packing your own nutritious food.

You can pack healthy food for trail riding as well. A sandwich case (and a flask, of course) are traditional hunt appointments that have practical applications. You can follow that tradition and carry a healthful sandwich with you. Instead of a flask, though, try a water bottle. You can even buy bottle carriers for your saddle on those long rides.

Avoiding Injury

Barn safety helps you avoid injury. Horses should be in cross-ties or tied with a safety knot to prohibit their running loose and creating the kind of havoc that could lead to an accident. You should wear proper footgear to prevent tripping or a horse stepping on toes in sandals. Electric fencing should be properly installed. And of course, always ride in a helmet, even if you are barebacking your horse in from the pasture. Make sure your tack is in good repair. Keep yourself and your horse safe at the outset, since accidents are one of the major ways people are kept out of the saddle.

There are a lot of heavy objects to lift at the barn. Hay bales, saddles, and feed buckets can all get pretty heavy and you should be careful when you lift them to avoid hurting your back. Remember the old saw about lifting with your legs, not your back. Instead of bending over to pick up that hay bale, bend your knees and lower yourself to it, then pick it up. Try not to swing your saddle onto your horse from overhead, either (don't rest it on a high stall door.) Pick it up in the same, bent-knee way or use a step to fetch it. Avoid twisting, and share heavy loads. Use carts or wheelbarrows whenever you can. Don't get too stiff while mucking stalls, either. Keep supple and keep an eye on how much manure or wet shavings you're trying to lift. (It gets heavy, especially the wet shavings.) Be very careful around farm equipment like tractors, spreaders, and golf carts. Don't drive machinery you're not familiar with.

Riding without stirrups can help you improve your position and make your legs stronger.

While riding, try to avoid slouching as well. It's not good equitation, and hurts your back. Same thing with perching, or riding with your neck stuck out. These are common bad habits that people develop often as an over-zealous attempt to "look ahead" and keep their eyes up. But if it's a forced motion instead of a natural way of being forward-going, you can make your neck sore and tense.

It's tough to find a rider who has not experienced some kind of knee or ankle trouble. Again, riding position has everything to do with this, as typically squeezing at the knee or jamming the heels down too far in the stirrups contribute to problems. But even the most correct rider will stress these important joints. Stretch them while you are riding by taking your feet out of the stirrups, rotating the ankle and moving your legs around in general.

Warming up and cooling down will alleviate the possibilities of strains and sprains. Stretching helps to alleviate sprains. Raising your leg to rest on a step of mounting block and stretching is effective, as are deep lunges. Also, you can take a basketball or soccer ball between your legs and squeeze to keep those muscles strong. Ride without stirrups whenever you can. If done properly (without pinching at the knee or squeezing with the calf) riding without stirrups is an excellent way to strengthen your legs.

Trying to improve your own shape and stamina will pay off in the saddle, but not all the work needs to take place on horseback. It's difficult to sit in front of a computer all day, then drive out to the barn and ride. Your horse, if he's been turned out, is probably better prepared for physical exertion than you are. While you're at work, try to sit straight instead of slouching over or back in your chair. Try to avoid being tense, just as you would while you're riding. Any practice being loose and supple can only translate to feeling better in the saddle.

Other Sports

It's hard to take time away from riding to work out. But often a workout will only take an hour or so beginning to end while getting to the barn, tacking up, warming up, riding, cooling down, and untacking your horse can be more time-consuming. Although it's a pleasure, the routine of going for a ride can sometimes take more time than you have in a day. But you can still be working on your riding even if you're not at the barn. As you're walking, jogging, or lifting weights at the gym, you're becoming a better rider.

When you find that you don't have time to ride, but still want to exercise in a way that will benefit your riding, try exercises like swimming or hiking that will help your wind improve and strengthen riding muscles. Other exercises may be good for using muscles that riders commonly ignore. Your doctor or a physical therapist can help you pinpoint which sports will be the most effective for you.

Yoga is good for improving posture and increasing awareness of body position. A yoga class can help you become more mindful of your body as you ride, as well as in what ways you are reacting to your horse's body and motion. Yoga can also improve strength, and many of the stretches learned in yoga classes translate well to pre-riding warmups.

Walking helps improve wind, and can help keep you limber. Some people include walking with their riding regimes; as you come back from a trail ride, hop off a half mile or so before you get to the barn and walk your horse in. Walking is also one of the easiest activities to do with children, and to work in during an otherwise busy day.

Remember that many barn chores provide exercise. Mucking stalls and leading horses to and from pastures offers a decent workout. If you're mindful of trying to get more exercise, you'll find many opportunities around the barn. Instead of using the farm utility vehicle or a golf cart, walk to and from paddock to ring to barn. Hike the fields as you check fencing or look for a missing bell boot.

Riding can be relaxing and peaceful, but it's also exercise. You and your horse are both athletes, and should both be in shape to get the most out of the sports and activities you do together. Then you'll enjoy your time in the saddle even more.

Gear | 8

From galloping boots to bit keepers, latigo straps to spur rowels, full seat breeches to custom chaps, the gear of riding helps us with every aspect of the sport. Items like helmets and safety stirrups help our mounted security, and multi-colored saddle pads and polo wraps are for fun as well as protection. Understanding the equipment required for your sport is one more step to becoming an accomplished horseman.

Tack

Tack is the word for equestrian equipment like bridles and saddles. Those are the two most basic items, but you may also find yourself using a martingale, a tie-down or a crupper, breastplate, chambon, hackamore, or flash. Each of these pieces of tack has endless variations, depending on your sport and the purpose the equipment serves. English nosebands alone, which constitute only one part of the bridle, can be flash nosebands, figure eights or dropped.

Shopping for and buying tack is one of the endless (and enjoyable, if often costly) parts of horse ownership. Some riders believe more in equipment than others. You may be convinced that a martingale, a leather strap that fastens to your bridle and girth and aids in holding a horse's head down, helps your horse to move better. Only experimentation will let you know what works best.

When you're thinking of investing in a new piece of tack, try to borrow it to see if it's effective for your horse. Otherwise, you may wind up with a locker full of moldering breastplates and crownpieces. Browse in catalogs and tack shops, but don't look to equipment to fix everything. A spooky horse may need more time under saddle rather than a shadow roll on his bridle. Even though tack can help, most training goals on most horses can be accomplished with very basic gear and work.

The two most basic and crucial pieces of tack are the saddle and bridle, and many riders never use anything besides those two items. Your saddle fits your style of riding—such as English, Western, or saddle seat—and your sport. There are different saddles for jumping, reining, and so on. (There are also all-purpose saddles, which are often the best bet for all-around riders.) While you can often ride different horses in the same saddle, improperly fitted saddles are one of the main causes of horse back pain and difficulty, so be sure yours fits the horse you're riding.

Saddles

Seek help when saddle shopping. A trusted professional or knowledgeable tack shop employee will be able to assist you. Most tack stores have vaguely horse-shaped saddle stands that you can sit in, and many will let you test ride a saddle. This may be a saddle specifically for that purpose, not the actual one you will be buying, but it is a good idea to take advantage of this if you can. Once you've ridden your horse in the saddle, you will have a good idea of whether you want to invest in one or not. Watch your horse's body language as you ride, because he will let you know if the saddle is truly uncomfortable.

You can do a basic test for saddle fitting with chalk. Dust the underneath of your saddle with a good amount of chalk. Then put it on him. When you take it off, you'll be able to see if there is chalk where there shouldn't be, like too high up on his withers or too far back. Or look carefully at the spot left by sweat after you've ridden. If

Saddle fit is crucial to your
horse's comfort and your
security.

there are dry patches, the saddle may be pinching in
those areas.

A saddle should rest on your horse's ribs, not right
on his spine. If you're sitting in it, try to work two
fingers between the front of your saddle. When it's on his
back without a saddle pad, you should see light all the
way through underneath. If the saddle is too narrow, it
will pinch him and he won't move freely. If it's really too
small, your horse may even act up from the discomfort.
While you can ameliorate some fitting problems with

pads, you can't truly fix a too-small saddle without buying a larger one.

If your saddle is too wide, it will slip forward. An oversized saddle will cause saddle rubs on your horse. Even before you fasten the girth, the saddle should sit fairly securely on your horse when he's holding still. If it doesn't, it may be too loose. Also, if it seems that the saddle has become too wide because your horse has lost weight, you can use a gel pad (a squishy, saddle-shaped pad that adjusts to the shape of the saddle) or back protector along with your regular saddle pad to rectify the problem.

You should be in the deepest part of the saddle. If your saddle is too small for you, you'll be out of balance. Sizes go from about fourteen inches for a very small child's saddle to nineteen inches for a large adult's. A saddle that is too small or too big for you can hinder your riding, making you perch or lean back to compensate. Make sure you're comfortable in yours. As you shop for saddles, remember that they are usually sold "less fittings," which means they don't include the stirrups, stirrup leathers, and girth.

Bridles

Bridles come in different sizes, such as cob, horse, and pony. Most English horses use either a cob or horse bridle. In Western bridles, most horses take a horse size, while some bigger ones take a large, and ponies and

some smaller framed horses, like Arabians, wear a pony-sized bridle. The browband should be long enough so that it doesn't rub the horse's ears, and the throatlatch should be fairly loose, so that when your horse moves his head and neck as he moves there is no tightness at the throat. The noseband (bottom part of the cavesson) should admit one finger below the horse's cheekbones. You want it to be snug, but not overly tight. Make sure all strap ends are in their keepers, and that you can slip one finger underneath the bridle anywhere.

Reins come in many varieties, from traditional leather to rubber for eventers and other riders who may have wet hands. There are even reins with rainbow-colored stripes to help new riders learn where to hold them. Reins should fit your hands. Oversized or over-textured ones will make you think about your hands more than your position, and too-small ones are tough to hold.

Bits

The bit, the piece of metal that goes in the horse's mouth, is another key piece of equipment. Unless your horse goes in a hackamore (or jaquima), which is a kind of bitless bridle, the bit provides much of the communication between you and your horse. It works by applying pressure, and should not hurt your horse. Like saddles, bits can be suited to the type of competition, but more often have to do with your horse. Bitting, the prac-

Opposite page: As you slide your horse's bit into his mouth, he should accept it. If he resists, you may need to check that his bridle fits him and that his bit is comfortable.

tice of choosing a bit for a certain horse, is an intricate art in itself, taking into consideration all the available choices and horse's needs.

Some stronger horses tend be easier to control when ridden in stronger bits, but many strong horses do fine in milder ones, like snaffles. As with other equipment, you will need to experiment to figure out which one works for you and your horse. A general rule of thumb is to use the mildest bit you can. If your horse does not need the extra control, why ride him in a kimberwicke? Start out with a basic snaffle and go from there.

The average bit size is five, but you can measure your horse's mouth size with a string knotted at one end, threaded through his mouth, knotted again, and measured knot to knot. The knots should be at the corners of your horse's mouth, and the bit size should be ¼ inch wider than the mouth. When you put it on, the bit hinges should not pinch your horse's lips. He should look as if he has a slight smile, or two small wrinkles in the corners of his mouth.

Other Tack

Listed below are some other pieces of tack and riding equipment you may encounter and how they should fit:

Breastplate: This keeps the saddle from sliding back with a yoke that goes around the horse's shoulders and a center strap that goes between his front legs. Then two other straps fasten to the dee rings at the front of the saddle. The center strap should be loose enough that it doesn't rub the horse's chest.

Galloping Boots: Also called splint boots or protective boots, these leather or neoprene boots go low on the horse's leg to protect him during sports like barrel racing or jumping.

Girth: The girth keeps your saddle—and you—on your horse, so it is very important that you examine it often to make sure its stitching is not worn. Girths are made of leather, string, or neoprene. Many people use fleece girth covers to protect their horses' tender belly skin. It should have a least two spare holes above the buckles when it's tightened properly. Always check the girth right before you get on, because many horses' girths fit more tightly when originally fastened than a few minutes later.

Running Martingale: This type of martingale fastens around the girth and then splits at the chest. Each strap ends with a rein ring, and the reins run through those rings.

Saddle Pad: Saddle pads go underneath the saddle to prevent its rubbing on the horse. They are made of a variety of materials, from therapeutic gel pads to basic cotton or wool ones. They come in a wide range of colors and patterns as well. "Baby pads" are made of lightweight white cotton, and can be used as an

You may want to ask someone on the ground to assist you with your stirrup length.

underpad to save wear on your other pads. Be sure that any saddle pad is placed smoothly on the horse's back, as a wrinkle will cause a sore.

Standing Martingale: This attaches to the noseband, runs between the front legs, and attaches to the girth. Then a rubber loop secures it to the strap on the horse's chest, so he can't trip on it.

Stirrups: For safety, make sure your stirrup bars, which are the hinged bars many stirrups rest on, are always kept in the open position. To protect yourself from being dragged, use either safety stirrups or extra-wide stirrups.

Stirrup Leathers: These are the straps that keep your stirrups on. You can punch extra holes in the leathers so that they are the perfect length, but be careful not to overdo this, as it does compromise the leather.

The moment before you mount is a good time to survey your tack.

Shopping for Your Tack

Since cheap leather cracks and stains more easily than its higher-quality counterpart, you should buy the best leather goods you can afford. Although good tack often seems prohibitively expensive, it's often more economical than replacing cheap tack. Also, lower-quality leather can be unsafe. Remember that you're held on to your horse by that leather. You don't want it to snap the day you've decided to go for a gallop in the fields. To save money, buy used tack. Or consider synthetic tack, which is often less costly than its leather counterpart, and needs only soap and water to stay clean.

Look for vegetable-tanned leather, which often comes from England, Australia, Canada, Germany or America. Leather with a pungent smell was probably not vegetable tanned. Good leather has a sweet, clean, "tack shop" smell, a glow, and a uniform appearance. Stitching should be strong and clean.

If you're shopping for used tack, remember that older leather, like newer leather, should still have that sweet smell. It should not have abrasions or marks on it, and the edges of reins, leathers and billets should be finished rather than rough. It should be pliant and not wrinkled. Most important, check stitching and straps for safety before you try used tack.

Caring for Your Tack

Your tack should be cleaned and conditioned regularly. Too many tack rooms are full of saddles and bridles that are drying out and cracking, or staying damp and getting moldy. The key to maintaining your tack over a lifetime of use is to care for it consistently. Each time you ride, your tack gets wet and grimy, and sweat and dirt can both damage leather.

Keep your tack somewhere dry and at a median temperature. A place that is too damp will allow mildew, and a place that is too hot will lead to cracking. Cover your saddle to avoid exposure, as well as unsightly scratches from the barn cats. Each time you ride, wipe it down with a damp cloth, and then once a week clean your tack, soaping it as well as conditioning and sealing it if necessary. Caring for your tack gives you an opportunity to look for wear and tear, like loose or frayed stitching. Billets should be strong and well-stitched, without widened holes or creases. Look at your keepers and stirrup leathers as well to be sure that they are whole and strong. Tack can deteriorate even when it's not being used, so check any old equipment over before riding in it.

To clean your tack, take all the fittings off your saddle, and take your bridle apart. Let your bit and stirrup irons soak in warm water while you do the rest of the cleaning. Remember to clean your nameplates and other metal fittings. Check metal pieces like the safety bars under the skirts. Some metals can react with leather and leather preservatives by getting black or green gunk on them. Clean any dirty metal bits first, since it's hard to keep the metal cleaner from getting on the leather. Once you've polished the metal bits, wipe any excess metal polish off surrounding leather so it doesn't stain.

To clean the leather itself, wipe your whole saddle and bridle down with a damp sponge or cloth. Terrycloth works well. Next, use some soap on your tack. Castile soap, oil soaps or any leather soap will work. Make sure to clean the crevices between the flaps and straps, and the designs on any tooled leather. Be sure that there is no soap left on the leather when you are finished, because soap will hurt leather if it's left to dry on it.

Remove all the jockeys, which are the black, gummy spots that stick to leather. Try gently using your fingernail, or something else sharp. Anything harsh, like most detergents, ammonia, and bleach, can harm leather. So no matter how filthy your tack is, only use gentle products and elbow grease to clean it.

Your tack will probably be damp when you're finished. Let it dry for about ten minutes before conditioning. Conditioning is the process of replacing the fat and oil that get lost in the natural course of using tack. How often to condition depends on many factors, such as what climate you live in, how often you ride, and if the leather has been subjected to some kind of stress such as getting soaked or dried out. Properly conditioned leather will look and feel even and supple, and will often have some shine to it.

There are many products that condition leather.

Various oils work, and as with soap, there are countless conditioners on the market. Most conditioners are made up of a fat (animal or vegetable), and have various additives. Many oils will work on leather, including olive and vegetable oil. (Avoid baby or mineral oil, however, which can undermine the strength of leather.)

Whichever kind of oil or conditioner you choose, be sure to keep your leather well-conditioned as well as clean. Leather that is starting to look a bit patchy or dry probably needs work. Be careful, though, because over-oiling will make your tack feel floppy, which in turn compromises the strength and thus the safety of your equipment.

Before conditioning, your saddle should be squeaky clean but slightly damp. It is ready to be conditioned— or "dressed"—when it is nearly dry. To apply oil, you can soak a soft cloth in oil, or paint a thin coat of oil with a brush. Don't get any oil on the saddle's suede knee rolls, because it will stain. It's better to apply a second light coat then to oversoak the leather the first time around.

You can also dip tack into oil if the leather really needs to be treated. Just don't ever dip your whole saddle, because the oil can get into the stuffing inside. Warm oil will penetrate leather more thoroughly, but warm it gently; hot oil will hurt leather.

Unless your tack gets soaking wet often (if you ford many creeks or spend a good deal of time riding in the rain), sealing is not a crucial part of a leather care program. If you want to seal it, though, you can use glycerin soap or a commercial sealant.

Blankets

The topic of blanketing is a sure conversation-starter in any barn aisle, as there are many different views. Some horses get by with no blankets at all, while others have one for every kind of weather, from a light sheet to a heavy-duty turnout rug. Blanketing is fraught with discord because what you do depends upon many factors, including your horse, the climate in which you live, and your method of horsekeeping. Blankets come in a wide variety, from water-resistant sheets (a sheet is usually a lighter-weight blanket) to super poly-filled rugs (the heavier blankets) for very cold temperatures.

If your horse is clipped, he presumably lives inside. You may have clipped him for shows, or because you ride so much in the winter that it would take too long for him to cool down properly if he had kept his heavier coat. A clipped horse will need several different kinds of blankets for different weather, including a warm rug for very cold days and a stable blanket on chilly nights when he's inside.

If you have a pasture-kept horse who is not clipped, you may rarely need a blanket depending upon the climate you live in. An easy keeper may not need one at all, especially if there is shelter in his field. If you only have one blanket it should be water-resistant. Horses are more compromised by wetness than by cold. They stay warm with the "loft" of their natural coats, which traps warm air and keeps them dry. You will sometimes see horses standing in a field with a "blanket" of unmelted snow, which acts as insulation.

Safety Equipment

You should always wear an ASTM/SEI certified helmet when you ride, even when you're barebacking your horse in from the pasture in a halter and lead rope. Riding is a dangerous sport, and no matter how trustworthy your horse is, there is always the chance that he will shy or bolt and you will come off in a harmful way. Activities like jumping can increase the risk of falls. A helmet cannot protect you from all injuries, but can prevent some of the most major ones. Even Western riders can wear helmets. There are cowboy hat helmets available as

Whenever you are mounted, you should wear a helmet.

well as the more generic models that many trail riders and endurance riders use. These don't resemble hunt caps, but have a sleeker, more modern look.

Safety stirrups prevent your foot from getting caught in the stirrup. If you fall, you won't get dragged. These come with elastic bands on the outer edges, or are hinged or otherwise shaped to allow a foot to slide out. Be sure that your stirrups are large enough for your boots, and keep the safety bars that your stirrups hang from in the down position.

Many three-day event and cross-country riders wear protective vests. These don't protect you from spinal injury, but do give you some defense against a horse stepping on you as well as any surface injuries you'd suffer from a fall. Fit is important in vests because in improperly fitted one will hinder your range of movement, so seek help from the tack store if you decide to shop for a vest.

If you ride in an area where people hunt for game, consider buying blaze orange accessories, such as helmet covers and vests. You need to be visible in the woods, as horses treading paths can sound similar to deer. There are blaze orange halters and blankets available as well, for horses who live in pastures near hunting grounds.

Clothing

Riding clothes have been used as fashion templates for so long that it's sometimes tough to determine who's actually off for a ride and who's simply following the latest trend. Jodphurs and tall boots, cowboy hats and bandannas are all seen on city streets as often as they are seen around the barn. Even in the horse world, much of the clothing is centered toward fashion; plaid schooling breeches are no more effective than plain ones. But like regular clothes, riding clothes are individual. Some articles of equestrian wear are more helpful to riders than others. Being reasonably tidy as you ride is considered a sign of respect for your sport and your horse. Appearance has always been an important part of horsemanship. Just as you groom your horse before you ride, you should be "turned out for schooling," or dressed neatly to demonstrate your readiness to ride.

English or Western boots keep your foot from sliding through the stirrup, and have hard, smooth soles to be more effective as a base as you ride. Hiking boots and "duck" boots have heels, but tend to be overly wide for stirrups. And sneakers are a bad idea on horseback because they don't have heels. If you don't need a pair of tall show boots, paddock boots are fine for English and Western riders. These are the shorter version, and either lace or zip up the front. They are traditionally worn with jodphurs, but people now wear them with breeches and jeans as well. Leather boots need to be cared for in the same manner as your tack.

English riding pants are usually either jodphurs or breeches. Both are tight-fitting (the jodphurs with the puffed-out thighs, although traditional, are not usually seen around contemporary barns on an everyday basis).

Breeches are traditionally worn with tall boots.

Children often wear jodphurs, since these are the pants to wear with shorter boots, practical for children who will outgrow the more expensive tall boots so quickly. Jodphurs have cuffs, and stirrup straps that go under the sole of your boot to keep them down. They also usually have some kind of textured knee patch, made of suede or a synthetic version, that gives you some purchase on the saddle.

Breeches have this knee patch as well, and if they are full seat breeches, it extends all the way up to your seat.

They end at the ankle, and are traditionally worn with tall boots. Nowadays, though, you'll also see people wearing these with paddock boots. Breeches come in every color, as do riding tights, schooling breeches, or schooling sweats, which are basically like leggings with knee patches. These are often made of a blend of cotton and a stretchier fabric, and are less expensive than breeches. They serve the same function for someone who does not need show turnout.

Western riders typically ride in jeans, often the kind with no inner seam to rub between saddle and rider. But many English riders ride in jeans as well. Any looser pants, like chinos, tend to rub. And both often wear chaps, which zip over the legs of your jeans. Off-the-rack chaps are often more reasonable than the custom type, which often have details and colors hand-picked by the owners. The design of chaps varies widely, from vibrant Western ones with fringe to the more minimalist schooling chaps with the traditional contrast piping and embroidered nameplate. Material can be suede, smooth leather, or exotic leather, all of which requires the same kind of care as tack.

If you compete, you will need appropriate attire for your sport, from the colorful shirts and matching helmet covers of the eventers to the coordinated ensembles worn in Western Pleasure. And of course, any foxhunting will require traditional turnout. But for the rest of us, wear what appeals to you. Leaf through a tack catalog and you will see all kinds of equestrian attire: t-shirts with horse designs, winter coats and vests cut for riding, dusters to keep rain off your clothes and your saddle. Acquiring and wearing "horsey" clothes can be fun. As long as you have a safety helmet and proper footwear, the rest of your outfit can be as formal or as lax as you like.

Have fun when selecting gear for your horse and yourself. Keep safety at the forefront, and enjoy the wide range of products on the market for equestrians and their mounts. Take good care of your tack as well as your own equipment, and it will be yours to ride in for a long time.

Index

ground lesson, 32
journal for, 158–159
mistakes at, 158
optimizing, 156–160
at riding academies,
  154–156
trainer assessment in, 30–32
trial, 31–32
types of, 157
volunteering at, 145–146
Longeing, 73–75, 179
Long reining (lining), 73,
  74–75
Long, slow, distance (LSD)
  work, 171–172

Manners. *See* Etiquette
Manure, hard, 101
Martingales, 203, 204
Massage, equine, 62–63
Medicines, 100
Mindfulness, 55–57
Monday morning sickness, 181
Mounted games, 23
Musical freestyle, 23

Natural horsemanship, 41–64
advantages of, 63–65
aromatherapy and, 63
bonding and, 51–52
clinics, 60–61
communication and, 45–48
creativity and, 57
defined, 41–42
demonstrations of, 43–44
equine massage and, 62–63
flexibility and, 52–55
herd behavior and, 48–50,
  136–137

horse communicators and,
  62
mindfulness and, 55–57
patience and, 52–55, 56
plans and, 54–55
riding bareback and, 59–60
round pen work and,
  41–42, 51–52, 57–59
tenets of, 51–55
traditional vs., 42
training exercises, 51–55
whispering and, 43
Nutrition
for horses, 110–113
for riders, 188

Overeating, 102–103
Ownership
economical. *See* Economical
  ownership
rationale, 142
responsibilities, 116,
  151–152

Parades, 27
Pastimes, horsey, 166–167
Pasture board. *See* Field board
Patience, 52–55
Pawing, 102
Pecking order, 50
Polo, 23–24
Polocrosse, 24
Ponies, 119, 165
Pre-purchase exam, 92–95
Psychics, 62
Pulse check, 96, 174
Purchasing horses. *See* Buying
  horses
Quick-release knots, 71–72